Alexander's Writings
ON
Practical Bee Culture

Edited and Compiled by
H. H. Root

NORTHERN BEE BOOKS

Published in the United Kingdom by
Northern Bee Books, Scout Bottom Farm,
Mytholmroyd, West Yorkshire HX7 5JS
Tel: 01422 882751 Fax: 01422 886157
www.GroovyCart.co.uk/beebooks

ISBN 978-1-904846-69-7

Printed by Lightning Source UK

Alexander's Writings
ON
Practical Bee Culture

Edited and Compiled by
H. H. Root

NORTHERN BEE BOOKS

IN MEMORIAM OF E. W. ALEXANDER by REV. D. EVERETT LYON.

On Saturday, Sept. 19, there passed from earth to heaven, in the death of E. W. Alexander, of Delanson, N. Y., not only a prince of bee-keepers but also one of the purest and most sympathetic of men who ever lived. For many months this kind-hearted man was a great sufferer from an abdominal affiction; and when the end came it was to him a welcome release from his untold suffering. The end came not to our brother as a surprise, but was the culmination of his expectation, and the summons found him with his spiritual house in order, ready to receive his well-merited reward. .

For a year or more he often expressed to his devoted wife the desire that the writer might officiate at his funeral, and preach the sermon; and when the telegram called me to Delanson for that purpose I felt that it was a·sacred duty that could not be ignored.

Leaving home immediately at the close of my Sunday-evening preaching service on Sept. 20 I arrived in Delanson the following morning, and proceeded at once to the house of mourning. Our dear brother had but recently purchased a beautiful little home, and it seemed a strange providence that he at only 63 years of age should so soon be carried from it.

When the hour of the service arrived, a vast throng of people crowded in and about the home to pay a last tribute of respect to one esteemed, and an honor to the community in which he resided. Though a great sufferer in the last few months of his life, yet in death his face seemed singularly peaceful, with just a trace of that genial smile that made everyone feel that he was their friend.

I felt it a great honor to be permitted to stand beside his coffin. and speak of his many virtues, and refer to his beautiful Christian character. After the service his three sons - Frank, Fred, and Bert - and his devoted son-in-law, acted as pall- bearers, at their father's request, and tenderly carried his remains to the waiting hearse.

A ride of four miles brought us to the beautiful cemetery at Esperance, where his poor tired body was laid at rest to await the resurrection of the just; and as I turned from the grave I felt that the bee-keepers had sustained a great loss in the death of such a friend.

May I be permitted to say a few words of appreciation concerning one who, as a bee-keeper, was a prince among us - the greatest Roman of us all - a very Gamaliel at whose feet we learned so much? Let me speak of him, first, as a man.

E. W. Alexander was every inch of him a man. Every thing that was mean and base he spurned with contempt, while every thing high and noble found in him its earnest advocate.

Like Longfellow's blacksmith, he could " look the whole world in the face," so pure arid upright was his character.

Singularly sympathetic, he had a kind word for everyone, and special sympathy for the man who was down and out.

All the years of valuable experience as a beekeeper, much of it the result of costly experiment, he freely gave to his fellow bee-keepers, and nothing delighted him better than to see the success of others.

As a bee-keeper remarked to me after the service, "He was the great reference-book for us all." Yet withal he was the most modest of men and, though deeply touched by Dr. Miller's recent note, that he, as one of the rank and file saluted him in his triumphant march to receive his crown of rejoicing, he said to his wife, "That was very kind of Dr. Miller, but, really, I don' deserve it."

Second, as a bee - keeper. Our friend was a truly great bee - keeper, not so much from the fact that he managed with his dear son Frank the largest apiary in the world in one yard, as that his management was so thorough and systematic, as based upon such a complete knowledge of the habits of the bee.

If for no other reason, his method of treating weak colonies in the spring, and other helpful suggestions, have placed the bee-keeping fraternity ·under lasting obligation to revere his memory

As a frequent visitor to his apiary I can positively assert that all the wonderful achievements ascribed to him were literally true, as he was successful in every sense of the word.

It often pained him that others questioned the merit of some of his methods, notably that of strengthening a weak colony by placing it over a strong one, but he would frequently point out where failure was the result of bee-keepers over looking some little though essential detail.

Every plan he suggested was the result of successful experiment, and he was actuated solely by a sincere desire to see his fellow bee-keepers succeed; in fact, the success of others was a passion with him.

What he has done for the bee-keeping world entitles him to a place with Langstroth, Dadant, Dzierzon, and other stars of the first magnitude.

Third, as a husband and father.

It has been my privilege as a clergyman to enter many homes in various parts of the country: and yet I must say that, for happiness, harmony and contentment, the home of our brother was an ideal one. He loved his home, his wife, and his children. On the occasion of a visit he related to me with much pardonable pride the satisfaction he felt in the fact that his children were all doing well, and that none of them had ever caused him a heartache. What a comfort this must be to his sons - noble, manly fellows, everyone of them and to his devoted wife and daughter! It is such sweet homes as this that constitute the bulwark of our national righteousness.

In closing I desire to speak of our brother fourth, as a Christian.

Brother Alexander was not only a Christian by profession, but, best of all, he lived the Christ life and followed the example of his Savior, "who went about doing good"

Our friend made no loud profession; but every body knew that he loved God with all his heart and his neighbor as himself, and Christ said this was the sum total of religion.

A few days before his death, his dear wife, one of the biggest-hearted and most motherly of women, played on the organ, and sang, at his request, his two favorite hymns, "Jesus, Lover of My Soul," and "Nearer, My God, to Thee;" and when she finished he requested that she sing them over again, which she did, to his great satisfaction.

The day before his death he turned to his wife and said, "Oh! wouldn't it be nice if, when the end comes, I could just go to sleep?"

Truly, with Paul he could say, "I am now ready to be offered, and the time of my departure is at hand. I have fought a good fight, I have finished my course, I have kept the faith; henceforth there is laid up for me a crown of righteousness which the Lord will give me at that day; and not unto me only, but unto all them also who love his appearing."

Among those present was Mr. N. D. West, of Middleburg, N. Y., who, in the past few months, has been a frequent visitor to the Alexander home, and who, like the writer, felt most deeply the loss of a true friend.

"E. W. Alexander, hail and farewell." "We will meet thee again in the dawn of the resurrection morning"

The bereaved family have the sympathetic prayers of the bee-keeping brotherhood.

Whatever provision our dear friend has made for his family is as nothing compared with the priceless legacy he has left them of an honored life. If I were to choose the epitaph to be placed upon the stone to mark his last resting - place, it would be this:

"His life was beautiful,

His work enduring,

His death triumphant"

Rye, N.Y,

PREFACE.

In 1904 we began the publication in "Gleanings in Bee Culture," an illustrated semi-monthly magazine, a series of articles from the pen of Mr. E. W. Alexander, of Delanson, Schenectady Co., N. Y. For a period of nearly forty years Mr. Alexander had been keeping bees in a large way, producing honey by the carload. He was regarded during a large portion of that time as the most extensive bee-keeper in Northeastern New York; but it was not till later that he began to give to the public the secrets of his success.

His first writings were so valuable, coming from so ripe an experience covering so many years, that, as editor of "Gleanings," I finally induced him to furnish us a short series of articles. So much impressed was I with the value of his teachings in practical apiculture that I tendered him a sum far in excess of what I had ever offered any other new contributor, and with only one exception did I ever pay any writer more than Mr. E. W. Alexander. After he had completed us his first series I induced him to continue as a regular contributor, and this he did with more or less regularity up to the time of his death, September 19, 1908.

During a good portion of the time that he was furnishing us matter for the journal he was a great sufferer; and his disease finally compelled him to lay down his pen, which he had used so long and so well in behalf of his brother bee-keepers all over the country. After his death there came an almost universal demand for those articles in book form. So insistent were these calls that we were finally prevailed on to pick out the best of his ideas, and we now have pleasure in presenting them to the general public.

In this series of articles Mr. Alexander gave out many useful hints and "tricks of the trade." Some of these seemed to be almost revolutionary, not to say unorthodox; and occasionally his methods were criticised as being "impractical and valueless." But in order to understand the man and his writings one needs to know something of his locality as well as his methods of management; for his forty years of experience had shown that they were in perfect harmony, and, so far as he was concerned, he had no desire to recall anything he had said. While at times he may have seemed unorthodox, yet it must be remembered that he occupied a locality where conditions were peculiar, not to say remarkable. He was the only bee-keeper in the United States who was ever able to manage from 700 to 800 colonies all in one yard. Others have had as many as 500; but this has always been regarded as an extremely high figure for one place. Mr. Alexander's apiary was located, and is now, in fact (under the management of his son), on one of the hills near the little town of Delanson, N. Y. It is probably one of the finest, if not the finest, buckwheat bee-ranges in the

United States. From the Alexander apiary, when the fields are in bloom, one can see from twenty to thirty white patches down in the valley and on the hills, to which the bees are streaming in countless thousands. Then the locality is remarkable for the large number of asters which possibly furnish almost as much nectar as the buckwheat itself.

While the white-honey harvest along in June and July can not be considered anything remarkable, yet when this is supplemented by the buckwheat and aster bloom one can form some idea of the possibilities from keeping so many colonies in one locality.

These writings are not published in their chronological order, but, rather, have been rearranged with the view of having one article gradually lead up to another. For instance, we selected the first article, "Taking up Bee-keeping as a Business." While this was written toward the latter end of the series, it served as an excellent introductory to that which follows; for it gives one an idea of the possibilities of the business from the standpoint of one who has had so large an experience. The next article deals with what constitutes a good locality; and so there will be found clear through a harmony of plan and method.

The beginner should not lose sight of the fact that Mr. Alexander did things in a large way. Some methods that are practical on a big scale would not be adaptable to the management of bees in a small way; but nevertheless it will pay any beginner to go over each article very carefully, for he will find he can pick out a large number of valuable hints which will be useful in making dollars off his bees.

It may be interesting to note that nearly one thousand copies of this little volume were sold before it was ready for delivery from the press. This large scale of matter that has been published once, shows in what high esteem bee-keepers all over the country held this Gamaliel of beedom. We may well sit at his feet and learn.

Medina, Ohio, March 25, 1909. E. R. Root.

PART I

Introduction

BEE-KEEPING AS A BUSINESS.

When our attention is called to some new line of business, usually our first thoughts are, "How much money can I make out of it?" or, "How many dollars can be made annually clear of all expenses from a given amount of capital invested?" While I will admit that these are questions of much importance—questions worthy of due consideration—there is still one question which is of paramount importance above all others, which, I am sorry to say, we seldom think of. That is, "Am I naturally qualified for that line of business? If so, then I have the principal requirement to success; if not, then no amount of study or hard labor can fully take the place of my inability to fulfill its requirements." Oh how many of us spend our whole lives like water seeking its level, and never find the business that God fitted us best to follow! My young friend, if you have any thoughts of taking up bee-keeping as a business, then think this subject over carefully before you invest much money. My advice would be to work one summer, at least, for some successful honey-producer—one who would take pains to teach you all he could in regard to rearing queens, forming nuclei, increasing colonies, wintering, and producing honey—yes, and a thousand and one little things which only experience can teach. In this way you could be earning your board and fair wages while learning your business.

In regard to the amount of money that can be made from bee-keeping, it is like all other rural pursuits—it depends to a great extent on the season. It is no get-rich-quick business; still, if rightly followed, it will give as good returns one year with another as any business of a rural nature, considering the amount of capital invested and labor required. About five dollars per colony, spring count, clear of all expenses, is a moderate estimate of the profit from the business—that is, if run wholly for the production of honey without any special care to see what might be accomplished; but if run by an expert on high-grade methods, then 15 or 20 dollars per colony can frequently be made.

Here is where the specialist has a great advantage over the man who divides his capital and time into two or more channels. These men soon find that they have twice or three times the trouble to contend with, and only a third or a half the capital to use in making a success of any one of the several lines they have taken up; but the lack of necessary capital is only a small factor, for that can be got at the bank. But the necessary intellect, business capacity, and experience can not be borrowed, and without these elements to success there is only one alternative, and that is and always has been simply failure.

Then there is another thing to take into consideration. It is pleasant to have a paying business that requires your time only about half of the year, and that the pleasant part, when you can be outdoors and enjoy all the pleasures of nature's spring and summer. With me it is a real pleasure to breathe free air unsoiled by either bell or whistle calling me to labor.

I will now take it for granted that you have spent one or two seasons in learning all that you could during that time from some competent person, and you still want to follow bee-keeping. I can not advise you to go slow, as some do. That "go slow" is a blight on any man. First be sure that you are right, then go ahead with willing hands and a good stock of perseverance ever ready to overcome the unexpected troubles as you meet them. Make up your mind from the first to take good bee literature; have good bees; use good tools and hives, and then produce good honey. Take pride in your business. If you have taken up queen-rearing, forming nuclei for sale, or increasing your colonies for sale, or producing comb or extracted honey, don't forget to look well to quality. Then advertise and let the public know what you have, and you will in a short time not only surprise your friends but yourself with your success. You now have a clear track and a light grade compared with what some of us older men had fifty years ago. We then had a hard time of it—no bee journals, no Italian bees, no comb foundation, no honey-extractors, no bee-smokers, and no market for the little honey we secured.

How different now, with our large markets established, where our honey is annually sought for, either in small lots or by the carload, and with our new inventions and improved methods enabling us to produce five times the amount per colony we did then! To me bee-keeping now seems like quite a good business. Still, I never advise one to take it up, not even my own sons, for I have always taught that, when it comes to choosing a life business, each one should choose for himself. While it is true that man to a great extent makes his circumstances, still it is also true that circumstances to a great extent make the man.

I am well acquainted with a man who was born on a farm, and worked hard on it for several years after he was married. He was temperate and of excellent habits, working early and late; but still his farm life was a perfect failure. After toiling in close circumstances for several years his wife's friends got him a situation in New York city. Then the scale turned. He struck a place that God had fitted him for, and for the past thirteen years he has had a net income of over twenty thousand dollars a year. I speak of this case to show that many of us are trying to make a success of some business to which we are not at all adapted; also to show the importance of trying hard while young to start right.

You should look upon your business as your bank; and whenever you can add a dollar to it, do so, and it will return in due time many fold. Take pride in having a good apiary, and remember there is far more in the man than in the business. If the bee-keeper in the future will take our leading bee journals he can, through their advice, shun so many troubles that we older men had to bear that it is almost like another business—not but that it is still subject to many discouraging conditions; and our inability to have any control over the season is and always will be its worst feature. But all lines of business have some troubles with which to contend. When the farmer loses his stock it is hard and costly to replace, and it often takes some time to do it; or when ⌐is crops are ruined by untimely frosts or protracted drouths the loss is hard to bear and overcome. But when the bee-keeper loses a large per cent of his bees he still has the hives and combs left; and if he has some good colonies he can soon have his original number again with but little expense, and usually secure some surplus besides.

Here is one great advantage our business has over many others. Taking our bees safely through long cold winters and very changeable spring weather, with small loss, has been a hard problem to solve; but this part of the business is now so much better understood by nearly all bee-keepers than it was a few years ago that we feel much encouraged in eventually overcoming other troubles as we have this.

Each year brings some new methods perfected whereby our business is placed on a more reliable basis than it formerly was, enabling us to produce honey cheaper than we ever could before. Still, we have some dark clouds of losses and disappointments hovering over us. I have seen many through which it was almost impossible to see a ray of silver lining; but as the mariner's compass will guide the ship safely through ocean storms, so will continual perseverence lead you on and on through the trying hours until a clear unclouded sunset welcomes you to a land of rest.

February, 1907.

WHAT CONSTITUTES A "FAIRLY GOOD LOCALITY"? IS IT BEST
TO ALLOW THE FIRST HONEY TO FILL THE
BROOD-CHAMBER?

It may not be out of place for me to describe what I consider a fairly good locality. It is this:

Any place, after June 1, that will furnish a harvest for 35 days, sufficient for one colony of Italian bees of a good honey-gathering strain to gather a surplus of 100 lbs. of extracted honey, is what I call a fairly good location, and is as good a locality as this is; and all that we have been able to secure more than that has been done by adapting certain methods which the majority of bee-keepers have known but little about until recently.

Now as to the number of colonies that this or any other fairly good location can furnish a good surplus for. That is a problem that no one has ever been able to solve. I know that this location has furnished and can furnish a surplus of just as many pounds of honey per colony for 750 colonies in one yard as it ever did for a less number, and I think the same will yet be proven true of any fairly good location.

In regard to breaking up good colonies just previous to the main honey-flow, I can say that I have never advised any one to do this except where *increase was preferred to surplus honey*. I have always advised doing every thing possible to build up the colonies so that they will not only be strong in bees but have their hives well filled with brood in order to keep them strong during the whole honey-flow. Either make the increase long enough before the harvest to enable all colonies to become strong in time for it, as can very easily be done in a buckwheat location, or make no increase until the harvest for surplus is over.

LEAVING THE WELL-BEATEN PATH, AND THE CONSEQUENCES.

In regard to the wisdom of cautioning beginners about leaving the "beaten paths too far, and following what may in their localities turn out after all to be a phantom," I wish to say that, when I was a boy, a very small minority of bee-keepers left the well-beaten path of setting their best colonies over a brimstone-pit in order to get a little honey, and adopted the more humane way of cutting a little out of the sides of their hives in order that they might save their bees for another year; and I could never see any phantom about that. I can well remember many years ago, of a small minority that left the well-beaten path of box hives, and in their place adopted movable-comb hives. There was no phantom about that either. Also a small minority that left the well-beaten path of keeping black bees, and in their place keep only good strains of Italians— no phantom about that. Yes, and a small minority that left the well-beaten path of squeezing their honey through a bag, and in its place adopted the improved honey-extractors of to-day. No phantom about that; and it has so happened that a small minority at one time left that well-beaten path of producing their surplus comb honey in coarse hemlock boxes holding 15 or 20 lbs. apiece, and adopted the nice attractive section of the present day—no phantom about leaving that beaten path, that I can see. I might continue to cite many more cases where a small minority have left beaten paths in all lines of business and become the leaders of progress. History shows us, in thousands of instances, where minorities have been in the right, and were a target for the arrows of critics who only followed in their wake and drifted with the masses.

June, 1906.

AMOUNT OF HONEY PER COLONY.

WHAT CAN WE REASONABLY EXPECT TO OBTAIN WHEN WE GIVE OUR BEES THE BEST OF CARE?

This is a question which we are often asked by those who know but little about bees, and I sometimes think it might be a good question for each one of us to ask ourselves, and then do a little thinking along this line. For some time I have been thinking this matter over, and I have come to the conclusion that I never gave my bees what might be called the best of care, neither have I ever seen a man who did. Now, why is this? Simply because we have got the idea into our heads that we must have a great number of colonies in order to make a little money. Now, this is a big mistake, and the sooner we realize it the better.

Let us apply the same management to bee-keeping that we see put into practice by all the successful business men of the country. They make the most out of every thing connected with their business that they possibly can. Is it so with us? I don't think it is. There are but very few who give their bees extra care, consequently their surplus is small per colony, and they may become discouraged. Now let us look this matter over and see if we can not do much better in the future with fewer colonies than many of us are now doing with several hundred; and, by way of explaining this matter, I will suppose that on April 15, you have 100 fairly good colonies that were just taken from their winter quarters, and that each colony contains a good well-developed Italian queen not over ten months old that has been reared from some good honey-gathering strain of bees. I shall take it for granted that your hives are filled with nice worker combs.

We will commence the season's work by putting a feeder under every hive and giving each colony about 1½ cents' worth of extracted honey, or sugar syrup, which must be made very thin, of about the consistency of nectar, and feed them about this amount every day that the weather is such they can not gather anything from flowers until about the last of May. This will require on an average, one season with another, about 50 cents' worth of honey or sugar per colony; and, if properly done, you will have, May 25, every hive crowded with brood and maturing bees at the rate of 2,000 or more a day.

About two weeks previous to this we should start the rearing of four or five hundred queen-cells, which are now, May 26, about ready to hatch. Now we will divide our 100 colonies, making two of each, and fix them so that the queenless part will mature two or more of these ripe queen-cells or virgins into nice laying queens; then about the last of June we will separate these colonies that have two or more laying queens, making 100 more increase, or 300 colonies all together.

The old colony, or the part that has had the old laying queen from the first, we have kept busy drawing out frames of foundation into nice extracting-combs, and we have also kept them from any desire to swarm by taking their combs of capped brood away as fast as they had some to spare, and giving this brood to this newly made increase.

In this way of managing your bees you have no swarming to bother with, and at the same time you have increased your 100 colonies to 300, and all are in good condition for any harvest that commences after July 4.

Now, what I consider a fairly good location (and no man ever ought to bother trying to produce honey in a poor location) will furnish a surplus of three or four pounds of extracted honey per day for as much as 35 days during July and August. This will give us about 100 lbs. per colony, or a total surplus of 30,000 lbs. from our 100 colonies, which we started with in the spring. This, at the wholesale price of 6 cents per lb., brings us $1,800. Then we have 200 colonies of an increase, worth about five dollars apiece, which gives us $1,000 more, or a total income of $2,800 from our 100 colonies we started with in the spring. Now we will deduct the necessary expenses.

First, $50 for the honey or sugar we fed them to stimulate early breeding; and there, my friends, is the key that unlocks all the rest. Then we have $400 for the expense of new hives filled with foundation for our 200 increase; then the matter of hired help will cost about $125, and the necessary barrels to ship your honey in will cost nearly $100 more, making a total expense of about $675. This, subtracted from your income, leaves a net balance of $2,125—a very nice income for less than six months' labor which is not very hard at any time.

Now, don't say that this is overdrawn, and borders on the visionary, for I know it is not. I have several times taken a few colonies in the spring and given them special care as I advise in the above, and in every case they have done still better than this. No, my friends, there is nothing in the above that is overdrawn.

The trouble with us all is, we try to keep too many colonies, and in doing so we do not give them the care they ought to have. The man who requires 500 colonies to give him an income of $1,000 a year is not half as good a bee-keeper as the man who will make that amount or more from 200 colonies.

Study your business so as to keep fewer bees and better bees, and make more money; also have less idle capital invested; and I know you will have less to worry about than if you continue as many as you are doing. I repeat, study your business until you understand it well, for I assure you that ignorance of any thing connected with our business is far more costly than all the bee-books and journals we now have.

Think this subject over well and when another season comes, have all your plans well laid on a good foundation, the cornerstone of which must be strong colonies early in the season; and the only way I know of to secure these is to stimulate early breeding by early feeding; then all the rest is easy enough. Don't think for a moment that I advocate taking any steps backward—far from it. I like to see men push ahead in their business, and make it a success, whether it be with 100 colonies or 1,000; but in doing so, do as our successful business men do—look well to the amount of capital you have invested; look close to your annual income, and then, with a critic's eye, look to the net profits of your whole business.

December, 1905

PROFITS IN BEE-KEEPING.

MODERN METHODS REDUCE THE COST OF PRODUCTION.

Some may take issue with my statement as to the net profit in the work—namely, $5.00 per colony, spring count, clear of all expenses. Well, as to that I am sure a very large per cent will question that statement, and I will admit that perhaps not ten per cent of the honey-producers of the United States are making that amount per colony. I will also admit that, during the thirty years of my comb-honey experience, I did not make $2.00 per colony clear of expenses from the many colonies I had then. Neither did I make $3.00 per colony clear of expenses in producing extracted honey during the first several years I was engaged in that business. But during the last few years there have been great changes made in producing honey. First, our bees are now bred from much better honey-gathering strains than formerly.

Then some have studied out and perfected certain methods in caring for their weak colonies in early spring, so we now have no more losses in that way, and we have certain ways of making increase whereby not a bit of brood is lost—not even an egg. There has also been great improvement in extracting and curing the honey, which has much to do with selling it readily at a good price; and a few of us have dearly learned the folly of all that out-apiary expense, such as keeping several horses, paying dear rent for a place to set the bees, and losing a large part of the working force from each out-yard in absconding swarms.

It is only a few years since it cost me 4 cents per lb., cash out, to produce extracted honey. How different now, with these improved methods put into practice!

According to our books, during the past three seasons we have produced 181,237 lbs. of honey. Now, when all expenses were deducted, such as hired help, including board, barrels for honey, sugar fed in the spring to stimulate early breeding, interest, and taxes on $5,000 capital invested, our own labor, including delivering on the cars at this station, we find the actual cost to have been a fraction less than one cent per pound.

Now, when honey has been and can be produced at one cent per pound, mostly with hired help, it is not far out of the way to state that bees will pay $5.00 per colony, clear of all expenses. But in order to do so you must learn how to reduce expenses to their lowest possible minimum, and produce honey in the largest possible quantities that a certain number of colonies can be made to do.

The fact that thousands of bee-keepers are not making $2.00 per colony is no disparagement to the business. The same can be said of hundreds of farmers in this section, who are not making net $100 per year from their farms. But there is no reason why each could not be made to pay well if better methods were adopted.

No, my friends, I don't care to modify my statement in the least, that about $5.00 per colony, spring count, clear of all expenses, is a moderate estimate of the profits from the business. There are those that are doing even better than that, as well as hundreds who are making but little.

June, 1907.

How that word "success" seems to fire our very souls with ambition! and we again and again think our business over, each time trying to solve some new problem whereby we can add still more to our income and at the same time reduce our expenses. There are two things that always bring success—that is, good seed sown in fertile soil; and that law of cause and effect which predominates in all things, affects our business all the way through. There is no question that bee-keeping, if rightly done, is fertile soil; and it rests with you, my friend, to inform your mind and adopt methods whereby you will become good seed to develop in that soil.

You undoubtedly have had experience enough to know whether you like bee-keeping or not. If not, then sell out and take up something else; but if you like the business, then "Stand not upon the act of your going, but go at once" with a determination to succeed. Work at it by day, and think of it by night. Aim high, and use all the skill you can command to make it a success; get bees of the best honey-gathering strain you can find, for honey is what you are working for; let all other things be secondary to that. If they sting, make the best of it. If they swarm too much, try to curtail it; but get the bees that will gather honey by the ton; then you will be on the main road to success.

THE DIFFERENCE IN COLONIES.

There is as much difference in the amount of honey that different colonies will produce as there is in the amount of butter that different cows will make; so don't waste your time on any poor stock. When you have the best, give them good care and you will be surprised at the results. Look upon every colony as you would an individual whom you had hired; then see that each one contributes its part toward producing a fine surplus.

After you once get your colonies strong in bees, keep them so during the whole year. This can be accomplished to a great extent by keeping only good young well-developed queens. See to it that they continue to breed well into the fall. This can be done by a little feeding.

WHEN TO PUT IN AND WHEN TO TAKE OUT OF WINTER QUARTERS.

In this cold climate I would advise putting them in their winter-quarters about the first of November before they have lost many bees by hard freezing weather. As a general thing I think waiting for a chance to fly in November is a bad practice. If you winter in a cellar, and can keep the temperature about 45, it makes but little difference how damp the cellar is, providing you have a good mat on top of every hive; or a good piece of heavy duck will answer if you have not the mats, and then raise them about an inch off the bottom-boards all around.

Don't take them out in the spring until there is something for them to work on. We have noticed for several years that the first colonies we put into the cellar are the last to be taken out, and they are our best colonies nearly all summer. Heretofore there has been about ten days' difference in the time of putting in the first and the last, and about the same length of time in taking them out. Now we have a new cellar in our bee-yard so handy that two men can put away nearly 800 colonies in a day, and disturb them but very little.

In regard to this wintering problem, in order to be successful there are a few things that must work in harmony together. First, good stores; total darkness; perfect quiet, and an even temperature of about 45. If any of these are lacking it may be necessary to give them a chance to fly earlier than we otherwise should, in order to save them from wasting away badly in the cellar; then when spring comes, do all you can to keep them warm and promote early breeding.

At this time they require man's help more than at any other time of the year; and if you expect to be successful, there must be no let-up until every hive is crowded full of bees and maturing brood. Yes, I mean all that that implies, and a great deal more; for you should now have a fine lot of young queens ready to make whatever increase you may desire; but if you do not understand rearing good queens then you had better buy what you need from some party that can be relied on to furnish you good stock.

DON'T BARREL HONEY DIRECT FROM THE EXTRACTOR.

Now as to barreling up extracted honey, as some advise, right from the extractor. This is something I can not endorse. If one is very careful it might do; but with some careless honey-producers it is liable to do much harm. Even if of good quality when extracted there will be a little scum rising to the top after a few days. This, if left in the barrels, gives it a bad appearance, and many times hurts its sale. Then if there should be a little thin honey in the barrel this will also rise to the top and have a tendency to ferment. Here is one of the reasons why we have always used large storage-tanks. With them, whatever rises to the top can easily be skimmed off; and in drawing off from the bottom of our tanks we get only the thick pure honey of the finest quality. We are sure that, in giving this part of the business special attention, as we do, it has much bearing on the ready sale we find for all we can produce. If you expect to make bee-keeping a success, you must look close to all these things. Don't be afraid to give a dollar's worth of good honey for every dollar you receive from a customer; for if you are, your customers will soon find it out.

BEE-KEEPING AND OTHER SIDE LINES NOT ADVISED.

In regard to running some other business with bee-keeping I must say I don't think much of it. If you want a larger income, just add on one or two hundred more colonies. I don't know of anything so nice to go with bee-keeping as plenty of bees. Some are so slack that a large per cent of their colonies give them little or no surplus. This is all wrong, and shows that their owner is not caring for them as he should. The idea of having 100 colonies, and getting surplus from only 75, is on a par with box-hive apiaries. It is now high time that we get away from that slipshod way of caring for our bees. Don't let one single colony sulk away its time. If they will not work without it, take away from them all the honey they have, and then let them work or starve. Sometimes we have swarms that have to be treated in this way. We don't keep bees for the fun of lugging them out and in the cellar spring and fall, and what stings we can get through the summer. We care for them simply for the dollars we can get for their surplus honey; and if we don't get some from every colony we know it is our fault. My advice is, just as soon as you find a colony that is not doing well, attend to it at once. That is your business. Either put it in a shape so that in a few days it will be all right, or unite it with another. If you don't want to do this, put it with your nuclei, and consider it one of them. I frequently find bee-keepers who allow far too much drone comb in their hives. It is certainly much better to restrict the rearing of drones to two or three colonies than to allow many thousand drones to be reared in the place of worker bees. This one thing of itself often makes the difference of several pounds of surplus in many of our colonies. It will pay you well to bear this in mind.

My friends, in the above you will find a few of the many necessary things spoken of that make bee-keeping a success. Please weigh each one separately, and in doing so make all the improvements you can; for it is my hope that you will some day enjoy success in bee-keeping.

Delanson, N. Y.

July,1906.

THE CONDITIONS THAT CONTROL THE FLOW OF NECTAR; THE SEASON MORE IMPORTANT THAN THE AMOUNT OF BLOOM; OVERSTOCKING; PREPARING FOR WINTER IN JULY.

OUR LOCATION.

In regard to this location, let me say that we seldom get any surplus until August. Of the 19 years that I have kept bees here there have been only four seasons when we got any surplus honey until our buckwheat harvest; but this season we got a fine lot of light honey in June and July; but when our buckwheat harvest commenced the weather turned cool, cloudy, and wet, so the bees could find honey only a day or two at a time, although there were thousands of acres of buckwheat in full bloom within two or three miles of them. Still, we have had about an average season. The largest yield we have ever had was 149½ lbs. per colony, spring count. That was an exceptionally good year. This year, since weighing up our honey, we find we have 141½ lbs. per colony, spring count, or a total yield of a little over 70,700 lbs. extracted honey from this one yard, including 80 sections of comb honey. In addition we have had 3,600 sheets of foundation drawn out into nice extracting-combs.

To me the success of this large apiary this ordinary season goes a long way to show that I am not so much in the wrong in regard to over-stocking as some people think, and I am sure I should have to have more than 1,000 colonies before I would go to the trouble of putting any in outyards away from home.

November, 1904.

BUCKWHEAT AS A HONEY-PRODUCER.

During the time that buckwheat is in bloom, many other honey-producing flowers are also secreting nectar, principally goldenrod, which yields a dark honey resembling buckwheat very much, and with us is a better honey-producer than buckwheat.

Several years ago I kept nearly 200 colonies in a location where there was barely 100 acres of buckwheat within reach of my bees—that is, within four miles, or in a circle eight miles in diameter. Still, with this small acreage per colony it was no uncommon thing to harvest a surplus of 15 to 20 lbs. of nice buckwheat section honey per colony. This caused me to feel very anxious to keep bees in a buckwheat loca-tion where thousands of acres was raised annually, so I moved to this place. But I soon found out, to my sorrow, that the amount of bloom had but little bearing on the amount of surplus I obtained, and in this respect buckwheat is no exception to other flowers, aside from the fact that it does its best when we have quite cool nights followed by a clear sky and a bright hot sun with little or no wind; then from about 9 o'clock in the morning until 2 in the afternoon it secretes nectar very fast. We seldom find a bee at work on it much earlier or later in the day. But on goldenrod they will work from seven in the morning until after 5 in the afternoon. It also requires quite cool nights and a very bright sun during the day. Neither it nor buckwheat amounts to much in cloudy weather, even if the day is warm. With a temperature below 70 degrees on a cloudy day, bees will waste away fast on either golden-rod or buckwheat. They simply crawl around, unable to fly; and unless they get a bright sun the next day they soon die.

This question has a close bearing on the subject of overstocking, and it is hard to answer it without touching somewhat on that question. From the reports given in our bee journals the past season, during the commencement of the clover bloom in several of our Western States, I noticed that it was all that could be desired; but as to the yield of honey, it has been in many places almost a failure, and we have re-ceived many letters of inquiry for clover extracted honey from some of the best clover sections of the United States. The writers of these inquiries state that, although they had a very large bloom, their bees got but little surplus.

My friends, the time will come when many will realize that what is commonly called the "season," which is, the condition of the ground as to proper moisture and the temperature, and the electrical condition of the atmosphere at the time the flowers are in bloom, will have a thousand times more bearing on our surplus than the *amount* of bloom or the number of colonies we may have in one apiary.

A few years ago, during the commencement of our August harvest, when our bees had at least 1500 acres of buckwheat bloom to work on, and were getting honey very fast, a heavy thunder-shower came down from the north about 2 P.M., which caused the mercury to drop 21 degrees in less than half an hour. Then this low temperature of about 65 degrees, with windy cloudy weather, lasted some 11 days, during which time the bees destroyed large quantities of their brood, for there was no nectar in any flowers during that time, and they were ready to rob any hive that was opened. We have but very little basswood in this locality, and two years ago the bloom was very light. We could hardly find a tree that had any flowers on, but still our bees got a fine surplus of over 9 tons of basswood honey; but the weather was all that could be desired. It was clear, hot, and very damp; the moisture of the air condensed on every thing that was cool, and consequently we got the honey.

One year we had the most profuse basswood bloom I ever saw. Nearly every tree was full of flowers; but the weather was cold, cloudy, and windy during nearly the whole time it was in blossom, and we did not get enough basswood honey so it could be smelled or tasted in our surplus. I don't know that I ever saw the buckwheat harvest stop so suddenly, with apparently little cause, as it did one August. From the morning of the 21st to the night of the 24th, bees got honey very fast. Our hive on the scales averaged a gain of about 8 lbs. a day, and we extracted a tankful of a little more than 2 tons each day for four consecutive days, and our men all agreed that there was more honey in the apiary each night than there was in the morning. But on the night of the 24th we had a light shower with a fall of temperature of 11 degrees. The bees were very quiet the next morning until about noon; then when it warmed up a little they were ready to rob anything they could get at, and there were thousands trying to get into our honey-house around the screened windows; and we knew from past experience that the honey season of 1906 was then drawn to a close. The hive on the scales did not gain ½ lb. any day after that fall in temperature and shower, although there was considerable buckwheat in bloom.

Then at other times I have noticed, when the weather remains warm without any rain, the flow of nectar would last until Sept. 5; but if a break in the harvest comes at any time after the 24th of August we at once take off our extracting-combs, run them through the extractor, and put them away for another year.

One year we finished the last work in the apiary for the season on Sept. 1, and our honey was then all either in the barrels or tanks, and we had little more to do. We always prepare our bees for winter during July and August, so our summer's work was finished until we put them into the cellar.

I might continue to write page after page, citing cases where the weather has nearly all to do with our securing a surplus, but I don't think it necessary. The one principal requirement in securing a nice surplus is, as I have stated, the season; but this, being far beyond man's control, will always make the production of honey a somewhat uncertain business. The bloom of 60 acres of buckwheat added to what other honey-producing plants which would blossom at the same time, would undoubtedly help 100 colonies very much to fill up their hives for winter and give some surplus. I should consider it quite a help to an otherwise fair location; but I can not see how we can ever ascertain any thing like a correct knowledge of what our harvest will be, or the number of colonies that will overstock a location. My advice is, don't make any debts expecting to pay them from your future crop of clover, basswood, or buckwheat honey; for if you do there are many chances that you may be badly disappointed.

March, 1907.

A FEW THINGS NOT TO DO IN BEE-KEEPING.

INVENTING HIVES.

First, don't spend either time nor money in trying to construct a new form of hive—not but that there are some serious faults in nearly all of our standard hives, but let the experienced bee-keeper remedy those faults.

MANAGEMENT OF WEAK COLONIES; HOW TO PREVENT ROBBING.

Don't allow your bees to acquire the habit of robbing. Hundreds of weak colonies are lost annually by this provoking habit which is frequently caused by the neglect of their owner. One of the worst features of taking our bees from their winter quarters, a few at a time, is that it almost invariably starts robbing. The colonies that are taken out first, and have had their cleansing flight, being well located are in prime condition to attack every colony that is taken out later, and before they become located the bees from those that were taken out first have full swing at their less fortunate neighbors. In order to prevent this costly and unpleasant state of things, where you have to set out your bees at different times, first contract the entrance of every colony; then as soon, as you find a colony that is being robbed, even though it is only just started, close it up and keep it so for several days; then if they have any brood, set them on top of a strong colony with a queen-excluder between. If they have no brood, and still have a queen, give them a comb containing brood from some other colony.

In putting two colonies together in this way don't disturb either of them any more than you can help, especially the stronger one. If you keep a close watch on your apiary, and treat them as above described, you can save nearly all of your weak colonies with but little trouble, and at the same time prevent your apiary from getting into that demoralized condition which they frequently do when they find several weak colonies which they can overpower with but little loss of bees.

A CAUTION AGAINST MAKING INCREASE TOO RAPIDLY.

Then the desire for more bees is almost sure to tempt the inexperienced to divide his colonies to that extent that they are almost worthless, either for surplus or to try to winter. So, don't make your increase too fast. If you do, you will not only lose your prospect of securing a fair surplus, but the chances are that you will lose many colonies during the following winter.

KEEP GOOD BEES AND PRODUCE GOOD HONEY.

Then don't be contented in keeping bees that are not good honeygatherers. This is the principal thing we keep bees for; and if they fail to give us a good surplus when they should, supersede their queens with queens of a good honey-gathering strain.

Then don't produce poor-looking comb honey. You have no more excuse for producing poor stuff than the dairyman has for producing poor butter; but produce a quality that you will take pride in stamping on every package of it your name and address.

SOME GOOD "DON'TS."

Don't set your bees in a place where they will annoy the public. Either keep them where they will not disturb any one, or sell them and go out of the business.

Don't allow drone comb in any hive except one or two, and see that these hives have choice breeding queens. There is no more profit in keeping a colony of bees where a large per cent of their combs is drone comb than there would be in keeping a poultry-yard of roosters.

Don't allow king birds, skunks, toads, and snakes to hang around your apiary. If you do they will weaken the working force of every colony.

Don't think that bees will give you good results in either increase or surplus honey if you neglect them and fail to do your part. The day is past when the word "luck" has any bearing on bee-keeping. The man who conducts his business in a careless slipshod way, taking it for granted that this and that will come out all right, is only fooling himself; and the sooner he realizes it to be a fact, the better for all concerned. So, don't try any thing of the kind, but look close to all the minor parts; and when you have united them into one fine method for practice you will be well rewarded for your study and perseverance.

Don't spend any time in worrying over the frequency of poor seasons, but spend your time in preparing your bees to make the most they can of any kind of season that comes, then you will be almost surprised to see how few poor seasons there are. We have not had a really poor season in 25 years, while some of my neighbors complain of a poor season nearly every summer.

SECOND-HAND HONEY PACKAGES.

I almost beg of you not to buy second-hand packages to ship extracted honey in. Don't use those poor packages. If you do, you not only bear down the market price of honey but you indirectly raise the freight rate.

Don't bother with starters of comb foundation in your breeding or extracting frames; but put in full sheets of foundation and prevent your bees from building that worst nuisance of the apiary—namely, drone comb. The man with a few colonies may have time to fuss with starters; but if you have many hives to care for, the sooner you cut out this starter business, and the shifting around the apiary of brood, the better it will be for your net income. The earlier in the spring you can have every hive in your apiary, and every comb in those hives filled with worker brood, then keep them so to the end of the season, the less reason you will have to worry about poor honey seasons and overstocking. We have never had a strong colony of bees backed up with a hive full of worker brood fail to give us a good surplus.

PREPARING FOR WINTER.

Don't neglect to prepare your bees early in the season for winter. This part of the business should here at the north be all finished before September 10. To a certain extent we are preparing our bees all summer for the next season; then when the final finish comes, the last of August, we have but little to do, and I am sure that they will winter with less loss if they have a chance to quiet down and are undisturbed during the fall months.

Don't try to winter weak colonies. If you are anxious to save all you can, then feed them syrup made from granulated sugar as soon as the harvest commences to close, so as to keep them breeding until they are strong in bees. If you attend to them in this way they will often be your best colonies in the spring; but if you can not do this you had better unite two or more together in the fall; for a weak colony in the fall is usually a dead one in the spring.

Don't try to winter a queen the third winter. I am sure it doesn't pay. She is almost sure to die, either in the winter or early spring; and if she lives she is so slow to start brood in the spring that you will have a weak colony until mid-summer; and it will require more valuable time to build it up than three queens would cost.

Don't fail to keep your bees as warm and comfortable as is possible during the first four or five weeks after taking them from their winter quarters. We contract the entrances of all colonies to ⅜ by 1 or 2 inches. In doing so it prevents robbing to quite an extent, and helps them to enlarge their brood-nest, which is very important at this season of the year. We also try to retain all the heat we can at the top of the hive. We put a piece of canvas first over the top of the frames, then a board under cover, cleated so as to form two dead-air spaces; then our outside telescope top, which is kept well painted so as to prevent any rain from entering the hive. You may think this is taking more pains than is necessary. We think it has much to do toward helping the bees to give us a nice surplus during the summer.

Don't put your bees into winter quarters that will subject them to unnatural conditions. If you do you will lose many colonies, both during the winter and spring. It is almost impossible to save a colony that has been poorly wintered. We may talk and write of the thousand and one different things connected with successful bee-keeping; but when they are all summed up the whole combined is not of as much importance as perfect wintering. We could make more money the following season from strong colonies when taken from their winter quarters if they were in nail-kegs than could be made from little weak sickly colonies in the best hive that was ever constructed.

August, 1907.

IF I WERE TO START ANEW, WHAT STYLE OF FRAMES, SUPERS, AND APPLIANCES WOULD I ADOPT?

IN FAVOR OF A SELF-SPACING REVERSIBLE FRAME AND 4x5 SECTIONS.

If I were to start anew I would try hard to adopt some one of the standard hives already in use, mainly for this reason: If I wanted to sell my bees and appliances I could find a buyer easier, and sell at a much better price, than if my hives and appliances were of an odd size.

But, according to my ideas of a practicable all-purpose bee-hive, there are certain things of paramount importance that would have to be embodied in it before I could indorse any hive to the extent of adoption. First, I should want a loose bottom—one that is not permanently fastened to the hive. Next, a telescope top. These are a great protection to the upper part of a hive from the summer heat and the cool weather of spring and fall; and they never blow off in bad storms, which is another good thing in their favor. Then I should want the frames self-spacing, so no two could ever, through carelessness, be crowded close together; and I would have them reversible, with some simple arrangement so there would be no special top or bottom. The size of the hive I should prefer would be equal to a nine or ten frame Langstroth.

In regard to the clamp for holding sections, and the size and shape of section, I think the Danzenbaker clamp-and-section arrangement for comb honey is far ahead of any other I have ever seen.

There, my friends, when you make a hive with all those requirements you will have, according to my idea, the best hive that has ever been devised.

Since I was invited to partake in this discussion I have spent some time in examining all the catalogs of different hives I could get, and

I find that the Danzenbaker hive with its modern improved appliances has fewer faults and more advantages than any other hive I know of.

The hive we use for extracted honey suits us very well; and as we now have about 2100 just alike, it would seem foolish and be quite expensive to make them over into another kind of hive.

FACTORY VS. HOME-MADE HIVES.

In regard to which is the better and cheaper, all things considered, home-made or factory hives, I will say, don't be satisfied and contented with poorly made hives of any kind. I know of nothing more provoking than to have a lot of slam-bang hives. Bee-stings can not commence to make me feel as much provoked as to find some parts of a hive left a little too thick or too thin, too long or too short, to fit the place for which they were intended. If you are a good mechanic, and have a good planing-machine and all the necessary fine sharp saws to do good work, and can buy your lumber at a moderate price, then it is possible you might save a little in making your hives and appliances right through; but unless you are so situated I think it would be much better to buy all those things in the flat from some factory that does nice work. The one thing which is of far more importance than the first cost is to have every piece in a hive an *exact duplicate* of that part in every other hive. This is where factory hives usually have a great advantage over home-made ones. I have been fortunate in getting our hives and appliances without much trouble, always living as I have within a short drive of wood-working factories where I could either buy the rough lumber or the hives ready to nail together, at a reasonable price.

Please do not infer from the above that I have not had any experience in cutting up lumber and making hives, for I certainly have had. Twice one hand has come in contact with the buzz-saw, to my sorrow. In going over this part of the business, it is not only the matter of hives but there are our sections, queen-excluders, separators, clamps for holding the sections in their place on the hives, crates for our comb honey—yes, even our queen-cages and labels, and, many times, our glass; for all these and many others we have to look to the large manufacturing plants. Now, why not go one step further, and, in sending in our orders, include the necessary hives, and have all come together in a good workmanlike manner, even if it should cost a trifle more, which I have my doubts about, and then for many years enjoy the pleasure of knowing that you have all your bees in good well-made hives? This part is certainly well worth taking into consideration, for it instills in us a certain pride in our business which no man can expect to be successful without. Don't for a moment feel that any old ram-shackle thing is good enough for you and your bees, but make up your mind from the first that you will have every thing connected with your business just as good as any other man's, and then work hard to accomplish it.

Before I leave this subject I wish I could impress upon the minds of all those about to engage in bee keeping the importance—yes, I might almost say the necessity—of adopting some one of the standard hives as soon as possible. You must realize that you will have strong competition in the future in producing either comb or extracted honey, and it will be necessary to have the very best of every thing connected with the business in order to compete successfully with those who have these great improvements.

August, 1906.

HIVE-COVERS.

HOW THE ALEXANDER SUPER-COVERS ARE MADE; RETAINING THE HEAT IN THE SPRING.

A subscriber wishes to know how the under covers to our hives are made. I will say that they have a rim ⅞ wide and ¾ inch in thickness, with a groove in the center ¼ inch wide. In this groove we slide a board ¼ inch thick, which leaves a ¼-inch space on each side of the center board.

The tops of our frames are flush with the top of the hive, so when we lay this cover on top of the hive and frames there is a ¼-inch space between the under side of the cover and top of frames. Then when our outside telescope top is put on, which has a 2-inch rim all around on the under side, and rests on top of this under cover, there is another ¼-inch space between the two covers. This, we find, makes an ideal top. It is warm in cool weather and cool in warm weather.

We also use, in addition to this under cover, during spring and fall, a piece of heavy duck No. 8, or, as some would call it, a piece of light canvas, over the top of the frames under the under cover. This helps much to retain the heat of the colony during the spring, as it furnishes a perfect packing around the top of the hive.

The rims of these under covers are mortised together at the corners, similar to a wood-zinc queen-excluder, and then nailed. They are strong and durable, and at the same time light and handy to handle. With the outside cover well painted, no water or cold air can enter our hives from the top during the spring season.

We are all learning fast that it is very important to retain all the heat we can during early spring. We also close the entrance until it is so warm in the hive on a fair day that the bees will fan the air at the entrance as they usually do in mid-summer. This causes the old candied honey to liquefy, and prevents the bees from carrying it out of their hives, where it is lost.

October, 1907.

PART II

Spring Management

TAKING BEES FROM THE CELLAR IN THE SPRING.

THE THREE DIFFERENT METHODS AND THEIR ADVANTAGES AND DISADVANTAGES.

Let us think over the many ways of taking bees from the cellar and see if there is not some one way much better than any other; for we don't want to make any mistakes this summer, especially at the start; for if we do, it frequently means spring dwindling, weak colonies, trouble from robbing, small surplus, and discouragement in the end. These can, many times, be traced back to a bad blunder made in taking our bees from the cellar.

I will first speak of the two most common ways of setting out bees, and in doing so I will call your attention to some serious fault in each; then I will describe the way we now do, which we think is far better than the way we used to do, and as many are doing now.

First, we have a fine warm morning, and we wish the bees were out; so, come on, boys, let us set out the bees, and out they go. We finish about 1 o'clock, and find that they have all come through the winter in quite good condition, and the boys say, "Oh, my! father, what a nice big fly they are having! I'll bet there are some hives over there in the middle of the yard that have two pailfuls of bees now."

"Yes, I see, boys; and since the wind has sprung up from the east, nearly all those hives at the east end are getting far more bees than belong to them. Don't you see how they head up against the wind? Then look over here at those hives at the west end of the yard, and see how very few bees are going into them."

Then I draw a long sigh and say to myself, "It is done. I have made a big blunder, and I can see only spring dwindling, weak colonies, and small surplus for this season."

My friend, I hope you have never had and never will have your apiary in that condition. I have been there many times, and I know well what the result will be.

Now we will take up another way of taking out our bees. It is this:

As the sun set to-night it had every appearance of a fine day to-morrow; so come, boys, I think we had better set out about 100 colonies of bees to-night, for we have a big lot to handle, and it will not be so hard to make several jobs of it. So we took out about 100 col-

onies that night; and after they had been out a little while they quieted
down so they did not commence to fly until about 10 A.M. next day,
then they flew quite well; but as it got some cloudy, and they kept on
trying to fly, many were lost.

Well, we think it is time that they were all out, so we take out
another lot to-night. These have a better fly, for it is much warmer.
But here is a new trouble started—nearly all those hives we took out
the first night are robbing these last hives, which are so busy getting
water and locating their home that they don't seem to know it. Well,
that is too bad. We are now, as the saying is, between two fires. Those
that are left in the cellar have been so disturbed by taking the others
out that they are leaving their hives badly, so I say, "Come on, let us
get all the trouble on one side. We will take out the last to-night, let
come what may."

This is done, and the next day happens to be the brightest and
warmest day yet; and, oh, what a picture that apiary makes the night
of that last day! Those bees that were taken out the first two nights
have commenced to rob this last lot as fast as they tried to fly, and
not only robbed them of a large part of their honey, but the call that
those strong full hives kept up all day has taken most of the bees from
this last lot we carried out, and now less than 100 colonies have the
greater part of the bees of the whole apiary, and they are so demoralized that it will be a hard job to get them righted, and I know we shall
lose one-half of our colonies this spring.

Now the boys proposed to sit down and talk the situation over, and
see if there is not some way that this loss and trouble can be avoided.
O, experience! thou art a dear school, and I often wish I could give the
many readers of GLEANINGS more of our costly experience before they
make the many bad mistakes I have made.

Now we will take up the third way of taking bees out of the cellar:

First get every thing all ready for a big job, and watch the weather
closely, especially after a few nice days, for it is quite changeable at this
time of the year. Then when the wind gets around in the east, and it
commences to become overcast with hazy clouds, and has every appearance of bad weather for the morrow, we commence about sundown and
carry out all our bees—yes, even if it takes not only all night but into
the next day; and if it commences to rain before we are done, all the
better, for we don't want any to try to fly until they have been out two
or three days if we can help it. During this time they will become
nice and quiet; and when a fair day comes they will commence to fly,
only a few at a time, and will get their location marked, so there will
be no mixing up or robbing, as they all have their first fly together.
Then when the day is over we find by examining our hives that nearly
every one has apparently retained all its bees.

Now we feel that we have at least learned how to take our bees
from the cellar. We know that close attention hereafter will almost
wholly prevent spring dwindling, and we can see a fair chance for a

good surplus in the fall.   There are some who recommend setting out their bees quite early, some time before there are any flowers to work on.   This I have tried several times, but never with good results.   I'd much rather wait until there is something ready for them to gather pollen from, as soon as they have a chance to fly.   Some may be unable to see how this way of taking bees out at night and all at one time can in any way prevent spring dwindling.   It is this: It prevents a part of your colonies from becoming unnaturally strong by receiving bees from other colonies that consequently become correspondingly weak.   Then these strong colonies continue day after day to draw many bees from those unfortunate weak colonies until they have but very few bees left.   I have given this subject much thought and attention; and while I will admit it is not the whole cause of spring dwindling I am sure it frequently is one of the principal causes of so many of our colonies in early spring wasting away to a mere nothing.

Years ago we set out our bees much earlier than we do now, and we frequently gave them rye meal to work on as a substitute for early pollen.   This practice caused them to leave their hives in search of flowers, many days when the air was too cold for them to fly in the shade, and so we discontinued it some time ago.   We now like to keep them in the cellar until the most of that chilly weather is past; then when they are set out we do all that we can to hurry them along until the summer harvest is gathered.   If those of you who have a large apiary to set out in one yard will try setting them all out in one night I am sure you will be well pleased with the result, especially if you can choose the weather so as to have one or two cool cloudy days before they attempt to fly.   In that way you avoid getting your apiary in that demoralized condition that is often done by putting out a part at a time.   It is easy to make these bad mistakes; and, if done early in the season, they many times leave their blighted mark on our apiary through nearly the whole summer.

March, 1906.

SPRING DWINDLING.

THREE PRINCIPAL CAUSES, AND THE REMEDIES.

During the first month after taking bees from their winter quarters there are usually more colonies lost than during the other eleven months of the year; and it seems really harder to bear the loss then than at any other time, for we know that, if we can keep them alive and in their hives during those chilly, cloudy, changeable days of early spring, we can soon have them good colonies for the coming summer.   While there are several conditions that help to bring about these disastrous results, there are three that stand out as the principal causes of spring dwindling.

The first cause is an old queen—one that stopped laying early the previous fall. Colonies with such queens become weak in bees during the latter part of winter, and, not being able to keep their hives warm enough, they are soon affected with dysentery, and, after they are set out, they waste away until none are left. This cause of spring dwindling can be easily prevented by introducing young queens early in the summer, so they will have a fine lot of brood at the close of the season.

Another serious cause is poor honey for winter stores. This is a more frequent cause, and far more disastrous than the loss from old queens, for the losses from poor winter stores affect all colonies alike, and the poor bees die by the thousands while in the cellar, and still faster when first set out, until nearly every colony is dead.

One winter I lost 417 colonies from this cause out of 432; but we can now prevent all loss from this source by giving our bees sugar syrup to winter on in the place of unsuitable honey.

Another very serious cause of spring dwindling is the desire of the bees to fly on those changeable days I spoke of above. This loss can also be almost wholly prevented by placing the hives, when taken from the cellar, so the entrance will *face the north;* then in addition to this have a shade-board so it can be easily placed where it will shade the entrance still more, and somewhat darken it. To prevent still further their desire to fly on cloudy days, give the colonies about a pint of warm sweetened water every night about dark. This will encourage them to breed fast, and at the same time prevent thousands from becoming lost on chilly days in search of water. If you prefer to have the hives face some other direction it is but a short job to turn them around to any point after the changeable weather of early spring has gone by. Please try this method, and you will find that the bees will have but little desire to fly except when the temperature is warm enough to fly safely in the shade; consequently the old bees are saved until the colony has a fine lot of maturing brood.

As experience enables us to cast aside the fatal results of spring dwindling, it seems as if we had taken another step forward along the line of progress. The cares and anxiety of another busy season will soon be here, and our plans should be well matured for the coming summer. Have you secured your necessary help and your supplies? Do you know how much increase you will make and how you will make it? Have you decided whether you will rear your queens or buy them? If you intend to purchase, have you sent in your order? If not, attend to this at once. I find that some of our best queen-breeders by February 25 have all the queens engaged that they can rear the coming season. These are important matters to look after, and should be attended to very soon.

You may talk and write about the importance of a good location, also of the knowledge and experience of the man in charge, each being very essential; but *to have a good queen of a good honey-gathering strain in every colony is of more importance than any other one thing connected with the business;* for if the colonies have poor old queens that can not be induced to keep their hives half full of brood we might as well give up at once, for we shall get little or no surplus, and our hopes will be blasted. We should continually try to profit by our past experience, not only in caring for our bees, but in disposing of our honey. Don't be satisfied with the results of the past, but strive to make the coming season the most profitable one you have ever had.

April, 1908.

THE ALEXANDER PLAN FOR BUILDING UP WEAK COLONIES.

SOME VALUABLE HINTS CONCERNING STIMULATION TO INDUCE EARLY BREEDING.

The early spring is one of the most important seasons of the year to the honey-producer, for if he neglects his bees at this time it is almost impossible for him to obtain any surplus from his early harvest. We should care for our bees so as to gain two or three weeks' time instead of losing any precious days. First, I wish to call your atten- tion to the importance of keeping your bees as warm as possible all through the spring. If you can, try to have them set where they will have a natural windbreak of some kind. This is very essential to pro- tect them from the cold northwest winds; and at all times of the year avoid shade. There may be some places where shade is necessary in the apiary, but I have never seen a colony do as well in the shade of a tree as those out in the sun. During early spring I advise by all means contracting the entrance until it is quite small. We allow an entrance only ⅜x1 inch, and sometimes still less; then when a warm day comes we enlarge it according to the needs of the colony; then toward night close it again if it is likely to turn cold. Also cover your hives with tarred building-paper. This is an excellent thing to retain the heat from the sun during the day, and in this way you can, with the natural heat of the colony, keep the whole hive so it will remain nice and comfortable all night.

Then if you will do as I advise in the above, so far as keeping them warm is concerned they will gain fully three weeks' time over the way they are generally cared for.

Now we will take up the next most important part of spring man- agement, that of stimulative feeding. This, with its twin brother, keep- ing them warm, is the magic word that unlocks the door to a successful summer. I care not how much old capped honey a colony may have, there is nothing that can be done to your bees during early spring that will pay like keeping them warm, night and day, and feeding a little warm syrup daily, made very thin from honey or granulated sugar, or both. If fed in the feeders I invented a few years ago a very little will answer the desired purpose. Two cents' worth per day, or about

50 cents' worth if judiciously used, will be enough to carry the colony through the whole spring, and will, many times, be the means of giving you a large increase of colonies long before your harvest for surplus honey commences.

The rearing of early queens is very important; also early drones. This part of our business has been made very easy and plain by such men as Pratt, and I will pass it for the present. But there is one thing I must describe, and that is the proper and best way to care for our little weak colonies after taking them from their winter quarters. It is this: As soon as they have some uncapped brood in their hives, take them to a good strong colony; remove its cover and put a queen-excluder in its place, then set the weak one on top of the excluder and close up all entrances to the weak colony, except what they have through the excluder, down into the strong colony below. Leave them in this way together four or five weeks; then separate them and you will have two good colonies and will have saved yourself all worry about these weak colonies being robbed, chilled, or starved. When we are feeding the other colonies we usually give these a few spoonfuls of the warm syrup in a comb next their brood. This encourages them; and if there is not more than a cupful of bees they don't get much from the feeder under the strong colony. I have explained at bee conventions this way of saving these little colonies, and have received very complimentary letters afterward from prominent bee-keepers, saying that this idea was worth more than $100 to them.

This is something we have been practicing for more than twenty years. Some seasons we have a large number of weak colonies on top of strong ones during early spring, and we don't lose five per cent of them. I am sure it goes a long way toward preventing spring dwindling.

I think I have shown you how we can keep our bees warm and comfortable through the sudden changes of early spring; also how we can stimulate them to early breeding by keeping them warm and feeding a little thin syrup every day. This is very important; and how you may save those little weak colonies and have them ready for your early harvest.

March, 1906.

WHY SOME FAILED WITH THE PLAN FOR BUILDING UP WEAK COLONIES.

For the benefit of a few bee-keepers who have made a failure of this method, and also for the benefit of a very large number of new subscribers to GLEANINGS, I will rewrite this method in question, and make it as plain as I can.

About six or seven days after taking your bees from their winter quarters, pick out and mark all your weak colonies, also your strongest ones, marking an equal number of each; then all weak colonies that have a patch of brood in one comb about as large as your hand. Set all such on top of a strong colony with a queen-excluder between, closing up entrances to the weak colony except through the excluder. Then there are those that are very weak that have only a queen, and perhaps not more than a handful of bees with no brood. Fix these last named in *this* way: Go to the strong colony you wish to set them over, and get a frame of brood with its adhering bees, being sure not to take their queen; then put the queen of the weak colony on this comb with the strange bees, and put it into the weak hive; leave them in this way about half a day, then set them on top of a strong colony where you got the brood with a queen-excluder between. Do all this with a little smoke, and avoid exciting the strong colony in any way. If a cool day, and the bees are not flying, I usually leave the strong colony uncovered, except with the excluder, for a few hours before setting on the weak colony. The whole thing should be done as quietly as possible, so that neither colony hardly realizes that it has been touched. When the weak colony has been given some brood, and put on top in this careful and still manner, hardly one queen in a hundred will be lost, and in about thirty days each hive will be crowded with bees and maturing brood. Then when you wish to separate them, set the strongest colony on a new stand and give it also some of the bees from the hive that is left on the old stand, as a few of the working force will return to the old location, especially if they are black bees or degenerate Italians.

In every case that has come to my notice where this method has been reported a failure it has been by one of two causes—either from lack of brood in a weak colony to hold the queen and her few bees in the upper hive, or by smoking the strong colony so that, as soon as the weak one was set on top, the bees from below would rush up and sting every thing above. Therefore avoid using smoke or doing any thing that will excite the strong colony.

If done in a careful manner the bees in the lower hive never seem to realize that any strangers have been put above them, and they will all work in harmony together.

November, 1906.

SOME QUESTIONS ANSWERED

In reply to several questions regarding our method of caring for weak colonies shortly after taking them from their winter quarters, I can only repeat what I have already written upon this subject; that is, after the weak colonies have a little uncapped brood set them on top of a strong colony with a queen-excluding honey-board between, and close all entrances except what they have through the excluder. This we do about five days after they are taken from the cellar, and the bees seem to locate again so but few if any are lost. The very few old bees that may be lost by this method are merely nothing compared with the gain in bees after both queens have been laying three weeks or more. This is, without any exception, the best and most practical way of caring for those little weak colonies in early spring that has ever been made public.

Another question that many are asking is, "What becomes of the drones that are shut up in the old hive when increase is made?" As I recommended in one of my former articles, first, we have but very few drones in our apiary. I never thought they added much to the surplus honey of a colony, and have often wondered why some bee-keepers rear millions of them in the place of workers; and for that reason it doesn't hurt our feelings if we can trap them in an upper hive until they are dead. The bees usually pull them to pieces and drag the most of them down through the excluder. The man who now allows his bees to rear thousands of useless drones is but one very short step in advance of the man who keeps his bees in box hives. I am sure we secure at least three tons of honey a year more than we should if we allowed our bees to rear drones as some do. In the first place, it requires far more food than it does to rear workers; and then when you consider the advantage of having nearly all the bees in a hive producers instead of one-fourth or more only consumers, it counts much in securing surplus. So far as we can prevent we allow only one or two colonies to rear a few, which I think is all that is necessary for any apiary.

April, 1906.

BROOD-REARING IN THE SPRING.

HOW TO BUILD UP THE COLONIES RAPIDLY; EXTRACTING SEALED HONEY IN
MAY FROM THE BROOD-NEST TO MAKE ROOM FOR BROOD-REARING;
BROOD-COMBS OF HONEY NOT DESIRABLE FOR
SPRING FEEDING.

According to our experience along this line I very decidedly differ with some honey-producers, and say, "Yes, it is not only advisable, but it is of as much importance as any other one thing connected with late spring management." In preparing our bees for the summer harvest there are two things which should never be overlooked:

1. Every hive should contain a sufficient amount of good worker comb for a large well-shaped brood-nest; 2. A good prolific queen.

We think it pays us to kill many queens during the summer, without any regard to their age, simply if they are not as prolific as they should be, or if their bees are not as good honey-gatherers as they might be, or if they are inclined to be cross and vicious when working among them. It is not advisable to keep bees that have any serious faults.

Let us consider the brood-nest as one of the principal things connected with securing a good surplus. Until the last few years we took the advice of some writers on this subject, and saved a large number of heavy combs to give our bees during the spring, to increase early breeding; but with very few exceptions these heavy combs inserted near the brood about May 1 did far more harm than good. If we uncapped them it was sure to start a bad case of robbing; if they were left capped, then they simply formed a division-board which prevented the queen from spreading her brood across the hive, and, consequently, we had a small brood-nest which gave us a small colony during the entire summer.

After realizing the folly of this erroneous method of spring feeding we commenced to extract all capped honey from the brood-nest about May 1, and in its place, when necessary, we fed a little warm thin honey or sugar syrup daily for about a month. This soon gave us strong full colonies; and the best of it was, we soon had our hives packed with brood from side to side, and top to bottom. In this way of preparing our bees for summer we can secure three or four thousand pounds of old honey before fruit-bloom, and leave our colonies in 100 per cent better condition than they would have been had this old honey been left in their combs.

About 9 A.M. on a cool cloudy morning before the bees had commenced to work in the fields, I counted 237 colonies in the apiary that had the fronts of their hives completely covered with bees that had been on the outside of their hives night and day for many days, except when the flowers were secreting nectar; then it sometimes seemed as if twenty or more swarms were in air over the apiary all day.

Some may say that we should have put two or more hives of extracting-combs on each strong colony in order to have secured more honey. To those I wish to say that I never saw a colony so strong that it was necessary to have more than one set of extracting-combs on at a time. I have been all over this ground for 30 years; and in order to secure the best results, all things considered, I don't care to have more than one set of extracting-combs on a hive at any one time during the season. Now, do you think for a moment that such strong colonies could ever be obtained from hives that had their brood-nest partly filled with old capped honey, especially when there had been heavy combs inserted near the center of the hive, such combs forming a complete division-board through the brood-nest or a little to one side? When we visit our friends' apiaries and find only an occasional colony working in their supers, if we should take a smoker and open these hives that are doing little or nothing, nine times out of ten we should find that their brood-nest was so surrounded with capped honey that the queen could hardly find room enough to rear the necessary brood for a good-sized nucleus.

About the first of August a bee-keeping acquaintance called to see me in regard to his not securing any surplus this summer. He was a man of considerable experience with bees, and had fairly good Italians. He was using 10-frame Langstroth hives, and had in the spring about 100 colonies that had wintered well, and was heavy in honey when taken from the cellar. After I questioned him some he told me that he had about 150 heavy combs that he had saved from last season to give to his bees in the spring to stimulate early breeding as some recommended. These he distributed among his hives, so as he thought he would surely have strong colonies ready for the first flow of nectar. But here he was disappointed. His bees would not work in the supers, neither for comb nor extracted honey. He went so far as to unite several colonies, putting the bees of from two to five colonies all in one hive in order to get up a working force. I asked if those hives were not crowded with honey which caused them to be weak in worker bees. He said he had not thought of that, but they certainly were very heavy. I asked him about how much brood they had. "Oh! not much," he said. Some had five and six combs partly filled, and some had only four combs containing any; but every thing was full of honey, and he could not understand why the bees did not uncap that honey and carry it above.

Now, my friends, is it any wonder that he did not secure a good surplus, and that he thought it the poorest season he had ever known? I can not understand why a man of experience should have allowed his bees to get in such a condition. If, about the first of May, he had extracted those heavy combs he foolishly put into his hives, and also extracted the capped honey that was already in the hives, he would have had much honey to his credit, and his hives full of maturing brood which would have given him a surplus of early honey. I honestly think a moderate use of the extractor through the latter part of May and fore part of June, especially when running an apiary for comb honey, would be the means of many bee-keepers securing twice as much surplus as they usually do. Here at the North, May is the month of all the year when our bees require the closest attention. It is then that we should care for them so that every inch of comb in the hive is utilized for brood-rearing that can possibly be used for that purpose. Bring your extractor into use, cleaning your hives of nearly all capped honey, and see to it that every queen in the apiary is doing her very best to crowd the combs with brood; then you will soon have those strong colonies that will give you a fine surplus, and at the end of the season you will hardly believe it when told that the summer has been a poor one for the production of honey. Spring feeding has never received the attention that such an important subject should. We have been taught that honey is the proper food for winter use, and that, if a colony were short of it in the spring, just give them a heavy comb, and that was all that was necessary to do through the whole spring season. But experience has taught many of us that honey is not the best winter food, and that to give our bees heavy combs of old capped honey in the spring is one of the poorest ways imaginable to stimulate early breeding.

In conclusion, I repeat that a moderate use of the honey-extractor during early summer is very beneficial in preparing bees for the summer harvest.

November, 1907.

SPRING FEEDING.

Feeding is becoming a very important part of our business, and from the many letters of inquiry I am receiving from parties in many places I find some bee-keepers have rather erroneous ideas of the proper way to do this work in order to secure the best results, and at the same time avoid all danger of the feed entering the supers. There is no question but that we can secure very beneficial results by judicious feeding in early spring as well as late in the fall; but we must be careful to do it so no possible harm can come from the practice. I would advise having every thing as handy as possible before commencing this line of work; for after it is commenced there should be no stop until the weather becomes warm and settled, except on fair days, when the bees can gather nectar from the flowers.

Before taking our bees from the cellar we have our feeders all ready, and the necessary barrels of sugar for spring use in our bee-house; then with an agricultural boiler which holds 45 gallons two men can make the necessary syrup and feed six or seven hundred colonies in less time than we could formerly feed fifty. It is the advantage secured from taking these short cuts on both time and expense that I have called your attention to so often.

There are only a few conditions a colony is likely to be in when it is necessary to resort to feeding. First, in the spring, if the bees have little or no honey they should be fed at once five or six barrels to prevent starving. This syrup should be about the consistency of good honey; then to stimulate brood-rearing it is far better to feed a much thinner syrup. I find that, if made of 1 lb. of sugar to 3 lbs. of water, it will give the best results. This furnishes both food and water mixed together, which is very necessary to encourage early breeding.

When feeding at any time or for any purpose we must use good judgment; otherwise we may thwart the very object we wish to achieve. First we must be very careful to feed just enough, and no more than the necessary amount to secure the desired object. When feeding in the spring, give only enough for daily use of the thin syrup; and if there is a spell of a day or two that is fair, and the bees are getting some nectar from the flowers, then stop feeding until the weather becomes unfavorable for them to work, but don't stop unless you are sure that the flowers are yielding nectar. If you watch your bees and the weather closely you can stop feeding as it becomes more pleasant, so there will not be any syrup left in their combs.

If we gave our bees a lot of thick syrup in the spring it would be of but little use to stimulate breeding, as they require water at that season as much as they do honey. Then if we gave them the thin syrup in the fall, such as they require in the spring, it would be one of the worst things we .could do, as it would cause almost every colony to have the dysentery before mid-winter.

You may think that, if a colony requires feeding, it is of but little consequence when, how, or what it is fed; but there is a right and a wrong way to do all things, and our bees are certainly very exacting in their requirements. There is a great deal to be gained in turning sugar syrup into bees in early spring, and by it saving their lives during the winter; but remember, even if the law would allow us to do it there is not a particle of profit in feeding sugar syrup to bees to get them to turn it into either comb or extracted honey.

April, 1908.

HOW STIMULATIVE FEEDING HELPS TO GIVE A GOOD WORKING FORCE OF BEES IN TIME FOR THE HONEY HARVEST; HOW IT PAYS IN DOLLARS AND CENTS.

In order to acquire the best results from our bees it is quite necessary to do all we can to build them up into good strong colonies early in the season, especially where our main harvest is from clover. We all know from sad experience what the result will be if it takes three or four weeks of the best of the summer to rear a working force to gather the little that is left when the harvest is nearly over. So let us see what can be done in order to have a good working force in every hive at the commencement of our first harvest of surplus. I know of only one way to accomplish this, and that is by stimulative feeding from the time they commence to gather pollen until their hives are crowded with bees and brood. This can be acquired within 35 days from the time they first gather pollen, and costs only about 40 cents' worth of honey or sugar per colony, and a little time to build them up into strong full colonies ready for any harvest that may come, and is much better than to let those precious days go by and see your bees dwindle away to a mere nucleus.

THE ALEXANDER FEEDER AND HOW APPLIED.

With the feeder that is here shown which I will describe, it requires only one hour or less to feed 200 colonies; and in doing so you need not kill one bee nor waste a drop of syrup nor lose any heat from the colony you are feeding.

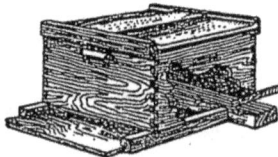

First, you see the feeder alone by the side of the hive; then you see it in position under the back of the hive ready to fill, and a 4x4 block at the end of the hive to cover the end of the feeder when it is filled and in use. We feed the thin syrup quite warm; and the heat and odor as they rise up to the cluster, even though the cluster may be only a mere handful of bees, will start them at once for the feed, and in a short time the syrup will all be taken out of the feeder and put into a nice circle around the brood. There is not any other one thing connected with bee-keeping that I have tested more thoroughly in all its different phases than I have spring feeding; and if any other man had invented this feeder and the way of using it I should not hesitate one minute in saying that it was the most practical feeder that had ever been devised, for it is as convenient to use in the fall to feed winter stores as it is in the spring to stimulate early breeding; only in the fall put two or three under your hive at a time, and feed thicker syrup, all they may require, at once or twice. They are not in the way if left under the hive all summer; and if we have a cold wet spell in mid-summer, as we sometimes do, causing many colonies to destroy large quantities of their brood, all you have to do is to pour in a little syrup once a day while the bad weather lasts, and you will save their brood, and prevent them from becoming discouraged. And, oh how they will work when the flowers again commence to secrete nectar! I can truthfully say that, with us, spring feeding has been the means of our securing fully twice the amount of surplus honey from nearly every colony that we ever fed in this way, over what we could secure when the bees were left unfed, and they had to use three or four weeks of the clover harvest to rear brood and bees to gather the little they could find after the harvest was practically over.

The cut does not show the under cover of our hives. This has a ¼-inch bee-space on each side, and it is very handy to cover over the top of the hive when extracting. It forms two dead-air spaces between the outside cover and the top of the combs, which is valuable both in extremely hot or cold weather. You will also see in the cut the entrance to our hive, and the blocks we use to close the same when we wish in cool weather, so only one or two bees can pass at a time. I wish I could impress the importance of this one thing, spring feeding, on the minds of bee-keepers in its true light; for I am sure that, if we give our bees the proper care in this respect, they will repay it in a bountiful harvest at the close of the season.

I am well aware that I am again in the minority on this important part of spring management; and I assure you it is not pleasant to stem the tide so often; but I find I either have to do it or keep still. I have only to recall the result of some feeding we did two years ago to show you why I am so much interested in spring feeding. We fed one half our apiary (250 colonies) about 40 cents' worth of syrup apiece, shortly after taking them from the cellar, and, although these were the lightest and weakest colonies we had, we extracted during our clover harvest over seven tons of nice clover honey from the 250 colonies fed, and only about four tons from the 250 colonies not fed. But during the basswood and buckwheat flow there was no difference in the amount of surplus these two lots of bees gathered. That three tons of additional honey that the bees that were fed gathered, brought us 6½ cents per lb., or $390, for about $100 expense in feeding, and I might cite other cases of the same kind. And then last season, in order to test this subject still further, we did not feed an ounce to any colony in the apiary, and our whole surplus was but little more than half what it was the year before.

You can make the syrup very thin after they get used to it, especially for Italian bees, as they will take it if it is but little sweeter than good maple sap. They require considerable water in the spring, and I think it is much better to give it to them in this way, for it saves many from being lost in search of it outside during those cool changeable days of early spring.

My friends, in the above I have tried to show you as best I could how you can feed your bees in early spring easily, and at but small expense, so you will be able to secure not only a much larger surplus, but also a much surer one than you otherwise would; and when this is accomplished it goes a long way in placing our business on a more solid and reliable foundation than it has ever been before.

April, 1906.

THE OPINIONS OF SOME OF THE AUTHORS OF TEXT-BOOKS ON THE SUBJECT.

In view of the recent objections to spring feeding, I feel it a duty I owe to myself and friends to call the attention of the readers of this journal to a few established facts along this line. We will now go to our text-books and see what they say on this subject. I will endeavor to be as brief as possible.

Commencing with Prof. Cook's Manual of the Apiary, turn to page 159, where he, in speaking of stimulative feeding, says, "As already stated, it is only when the worker bees are storing that the queen deposits to the full extent of her capability, and that brood-rearing is at its height. In fact, when storing ceases, general indolence characterizes the hive; hence if we would achieve the best success we must keep the workers active, even before gathering commences, as also in the interims of honey-secretion by the flowers; and to do this we must feed sparingly before the advent of bloom in the spring, and whenever the neuters are forced to idleness during any part of the season by the absence of honey-producing flowers. For a number of years I have tried experiments in this direction by feeding a portion of my colonies early in the season, and in the intervals of honey-gathering, and always with marked results in favor of the practice. Every apiarist—whether novice or veteran, will receive ample reward by practicing stimulative feeding early in the season, then his hives at dawn of the white-clover era will be redundant

with bees well filled with brood, and in just the trim to receive a bountiful harvest of this most delicious nectar."

Now we will see what A. I. Root says upon this subject. We will
take the first edition of his A B C of Bee Culture, and turn to page 75.
Where he speaks of a drouth cutting short the supply of nectar he says:
"Many of the queens stopped laying entirely. At this stage a little feed
during the night would start the queens laying wonderfully, and the
fed colony would rush to the fields for pollen in a way that demon-
strated at once that feeding at such a time was a very profitable in-
vestment if one wished to build up weak stocks and nuclei. A stock
that had been fed a half-teacupful only would go out for pollen an hour
earlier than the others, and would bring in double the quantity. A still
smaller quantity will set them to building out foundation most beautifully; and I never in my life saw the work in the hive go on so satis-
factorily as it did during the hot dry dusty days under the influence of
a very moderate amount of feeding during the night."

And then, again, on page 77, he says, "And after feeding perhaps a
ton of the grape sugar I am prepared to say that it is a decided success
for stimulating brood-rearing, for rearing queens, and building up colonies."

We will now take the late Henry Alley's Bee-keeper's Handy Book
and see on page 107 what he said in regard to stimulative feeding:

"When a colony is being fed, the queen commences to deposit eggs
more vigorously, and the colony exhibits greater activity than its neighbors that are not stimulated. Feeding for this purpose should not be
resorted to until the bees commence to carry in pollen as the effect of
the increased activity prior to this time would be injurious. The proper
time is to feed at night, and not over half a pound of food should be
given at any one time unless the bees are short of stores, and it should
be discontinued when honey can be gathered from natural sources.
Food for stimulating should be made quite thin with water, say six
pounds of sugar and five pints of water, and a small amount of honey to
flavor. The water will be utilized by the bees in brood-rearing."

I should advise making the syrup more than half water. I should
like also to call your attention to the latest edition of the A B C and X
Y Z of Bee Culture, and see what is there said on this subject; and right
here let me say that this edition to our bee literature is worth far
more than its cost, and should be in the hands of every honey-producer
in the land. On page 200 the authors say:

"In getting colonies up to good strength to gather the honey harvest, or induce nuclei, or full colonies for that matter, to cells for the
purpose of queen-rearing, the daily feeding of half a pint of syrup
should be practiced."

They also say on page 203, in speaking of H. R. Boardman, of East
Townsend, Ohio, that he practices a plan which often insures a crop of
honey even during poor seasons. "In brief it is this: He feeds all his
colonies as soon as it becomes settled warm weather, whether they need

stores or not. The syrup is given them slowly to stimulate brood-rearing. This feeding is continued clear on to the honey-flow, when, of course, it is discontinued. The result is that the hives are overflowing with bees and brood."

Then still further on the author says, "While it costs considerable to feed bees in this way I believe Mr. Boardman's experience has been such that he feels warranted in continuing it; and then if the year proves to be a good one he will get a tremendous crop of honey. One year when I visited him he had secured a fair-sized yield from each colony, and a poor year at that, while his neighbors round about him did not get any surplus, and all they did get was brood-nestfuls of honey and nothing more."

Father Quinby and his son-in-law, L. C. Root, many years ago were the first to call my attention to the value of stimulative feeding in the spring. They were very enthusiastic on the subject, and advised me to practice it every spring if I expected to make an early increase or secure a nice surplus of clover honey. I think you will find in Quinby's book, "Mysteries of Bee-keeping Explained," something on this subject. I have lost the copy I once had, and therefore can not quote his words. And now while I am in company with these shining lights of apiculture that I have just quoted above, I wish to be put on record as saying that I have practiced spring feeding for over 30 years, and during that period I have fed at least 5000 colonies for the purpose of promoting brood-rearing during the spring, and I am sure that, all things considered, it has been one of the most useful and profitable things I have ever done in the apiary.

May, 1908.

MAKING INCREASE VS. BUYING COLONIES.

BUYING BEES IN HIVES OF ALL KINDS AND SHAPES A BAD PLAN; DANGER OF
BRINGING IN FOUL BROOD; HOW TO MAKE EARLY
INCREASE.

This question is of considerable importance to those who have but few colonies and are anxious to secure a larger number as soon as possible. If we could buy good Italian bees at a fair price in the same kind of a hive we use, filled with good worker combs, then it might be as well to buy part of our increase as to make them from the colonies we already have; but this we can seldom do unless we buy of a supply-dealer. Then we can get a good standard hive with good combs and as choice a queen as we care to pay for.

If you want to buy bees I think, when all things are considered, this is the better party to buy from.

If we get our bees of some one who has never kept more than a few colonies and is anxious to go out of the business, then we usually get hives of but little value except for kindling-wood, and combs fit only for wax, with queens from one to five years old, of all grades, from fairly well-mated Italians down the line to the blacks.

But sometimes it is best to buy these almost worthless colonies in order to get them where their drones can be destroyed. In this case you had better Italianize them as soon as possible, then set on top one of your standard hives filled with combs, one of which contains brood; then put their queen on this frame of brood and put a queen-excluder between the hives so as to keep the queen in the upper hive; then in 21 days take out the under hive and use it as you see fit. Your almost worthless colony will now be Italianized and nicely transferred to your standard hive. This we find is the most practical method of disposing of those undesirable colonies which were in hives of all forms and sizes.

If your circumstances are such that you can hardly afford to sacrifice a part of your surplus in making increase, then you must be careful and make only such increase as will add to your surplus. This is an easy thing to do where the principal harvest comes in August; but if it is in June, then it requires the most thorough knowledge of the best methods of rearing queens and dividing colonies that have ever been practiced, in order to make it a success.

Those of us who produce extracted honey can make our increase much cheaper and easier than those who produce comb honey. With us we can divide our colonies in almost any way without seriously affecting our surplus. We always make rather more increase in June than we expect to put into winter quarters in the fall; then when a colony loses its queen, or is not what it should be, on the eve of our harvest we unite it with another. At this time we like to have every colony as strong as possible, and we care but little for weak colonies.

DANGER OF DISEASE.

One of the most serious objections to buying bees here and there around the country is the liability of bringing diseased colonies into your apiary. This we should ever bear in mind, and never take any chances that we can prevent. Then the trouble of finding bees for sale, and the expense of bringing them home, many times is no small matter. I have been all over this part of the business, and I don't care to try it again.

In regard to making our increase, it can now be done very easily since we can rear queens with so little trouble that it is easy to have all we care to use ever ready at almost any time. Then by stimulating breeding by feeding so as to have strong colonies ready to divide as early as our young queens commence to lay, we can certainly make our increase much cheaper than to buy undesirable bees; therefore I can not advise you to buy bees only in exceptional cases, but I do advise you to study well all the latest improved methods of rearing queens and making increase.

IMPORTANCE OF STARTING RIGHT.

You are the architect of your business—yes, of your whole life; so let no opportunity for improvement pass unimproved. Before entering upon bee-keeping or any other line of business, be sure you start right. My friend, did you ever realize the importance of those two words, "start right?" Teach your little children to study them; and when you see those poor drifting wrecks of humanity wandering up and down your highways in their abject poverty, tell your children that those poor souls which are now fairly steeped in vice and crime are the result of starting wrong in this life, and that only God knows what the result will be in the life to come.

Please pardon me in so often drifting from my subject; but when I think of that short sentence it seems as if I could write a whole volume on its importance.

THE RIGHT WAY TO MAKE INCREASE.

There are various ways of making increase. We prefer to build up the colonies to be divided until they are very strong in bees and brood; then when the division is made and the queenless part is given a laying queen, we soon have two good colonies ready for the harvest. We think this is a much better way than to build up nuclei. Let the same rule apply to making increase, as all other work in the apiary, which should be a harmonizing with your knowledge and the natural instincts of your bees. This is quite important in order to secure the best results. If we adopt methods according to their natural instincts then surely we shall secure better results than if we try to force them into unnatural conditions, which to quite an extent soon causes them to become discouraged.

July, 1907.

This subject has received, perhaps, as much thought and study as any other one thing connected with bee-keeping, and I will try to show that, with proper management, you can have two colonies, each nearly equal to what the mother colony would have been for the clover harvest, if not divided, and fully equal for a later harvest.

In calling your attention to this matter I take it for granted that you keep bees like myself, for the purpose of making the most money out of them you can, regardless of increase or the number of colonies you may have. Simply make what increase will add to your present season's crop of honey. In the first place, let me impress upon your mind the importance of doing every thing in your power, not only to build up all your colonies as strong in bees as you can after taking them from their winter quarters, but to keep them in that condition to the end of the season; for without strong colonies we can not expect much surplus. As the day is now past when natural swarming is desired by any progressive bee-keeper, we will turn our attention to some practical way of making artificial increase.

The most common way of doing this is either forming nuclei and afterward building them up into strong colonies, or dividing a strong colony at once by putting the greater part of the bees with their queen in an empty hive on the old stand and setting the old hive containing the brood away some distance in a new place. Each of these methods has some serious faults. The nucleus method usually requires so much time that frequently the best part of the harvest is past before they are in condition to take advantage of it. They also require much work and attention, and the other way of dividing the strong colony is all wrong in every respect.

I think I hear some of you say, "Yes, but that is about the same as natural swarming, only the old hive is set on a new stand."

I will admit it is something the same, though not half so good; for in natural swarming the old hive on its old stand *retains* part of its working force, and matures *all* its brood; whereas if divided, as is frequently done after its queen and most of its working force are left on the old stand, and it finds itself in a new place without its queen, the greater part of the bees that have ever been out to fly will return to the old stand and join the swarm, leaving the old hive with all its brood in a deserted condition. Then the few remaining bees will destroy every egg and nearly all the uncapped larvæ. Here you lose enough brood, many times, to make nearly a swarm.

After studying on this subject for many years, and trying every thing I could think of to prevent this loss of brood in making our increase, and at the same time avoid the loss of valuable time in fussing with nuclei, and at all times keeping every colony in good condition to take advantage of any unexpected harvest that might come, I hit on what I consider the most practical way of making increase of any thing I have ever tried or heard of. It is this:

When your colonies are nearly full enough to swarm naturally, and you wish to divide them so as to make two from one, go to the colony you wish to divide; lift it from its stand and put in its place a hive containing frames of comb or foundation, the same as you would put the swarm in providing it had just swarmed. Now remove the center comb from your empty hive, and put in its place a frame of brood, either from the hive you wish to divide or some other colony that can spare one, and be sure you find the queen and put her on this frame of brood in the new hive; also look it over very carefully to see that it contains no eggs or larvæ in any queen-cells. If it does, destroy them. Now put a queen-excluding honey-board on top of this new hive that contains the queen and frame of brood with their empty combs, then set your full queenless colony on top of the excluder; put in the empty comb or frame of foundation, wherever you got your frame of brood, and close the upper hive except the entrance they have through the excluder into the hive below. Now leave them in this way about five days, then look over the combs carefully, and destroy any larvæ you may find in queen-cells unless they are of a good strain of bees that you care to breed from, for they frequently start the rearing of queens above the excluder very soon after their queen has been kept below by the excluder. If so, you had better separate them at once; but if they have not started any queen-cells above, then leave them together ten or eleven days, during which time the queen will get a fine lot of brood started in the lower hive, and every egg and particle of larva that was in the old hive on top will have matured, so it will be capped over and *saved;* then separate them, putting the old hive on a new stand. It will then be full of young bees mostly, and capped brood, and in about 24 hours they will accept a ripe cell, a virgin, or laying queen, as they will realize that they are hopelessly queenless. I would advise you to give them a laying queen, as I never like to keep my full colonies a day longer without a laying queen than I can help. In this way you have two strong colonies from one, as you have not lost a particle of brood nor checked the laying of your queen; and with me it almost wholly prevents swarming. This is the way we have made our increase for several years, and we like it much better than any other way we have ever tried. In doing so you keep all your colonies strong during the whole summer, and it is the strong colonies that count in giving us our surplus.

The mere fact of having a large number of colonies does not amount to much unless they are strong in bees and are *well* cared for at all times. This is a fact that many have sadly overlooked; and when the season comes to a close, giving them a small surplus, they feel disappointed and lay the fault on many things that have had but little to do with their failure.

In making your increase in the above way your new swarm on the old stand is in fine shape for a clamp of sections, as it has a large working force backed up by having its hive nearly full of brood, and but little honey, as the bees have been in the habit of storing their honey in the old hive that was on top, so they will soon go to work in the sections and have no notion of swarming. Then the old hive that has been set away can usually spare 15 or 20 lbs. of honey, which can be taken with the extractor, giving its new queen plenty of room to lay, and in a short time will be one of your best colonies, and also have no desire to swarm.

Now, if you have done your duty by your bees since taking them from their winter quarters, as I have recommended in the above, keeping them snug and warm, and feeding them a little thin warm syrup nearly every day for the first 30 days after they commence to fly, you can have two good strong colonies in the place of one ready to commence work on your clover harvest, which here commences about June 15.

From an extensive experience along this line I find I can get nearly twice the amount of surplus by dividing as above stated over what I was able to acquire either by letting them go undivided or dividing in a way that caused the loss of a greater part of their brood. This losing of brood we must guard against at all times if we expect to secure a fine surplus. It costs both time and honey to produce it, and it is the principal factor in obtaining those strong colonies that give us tons of honey.

Far too many bee-keepers think that the value of their apiary consists in the number of colonies they keep. This is so only to a certain extent; for if you had 1000 colonies and they were all weak in bees, so they would give you no surplus, they would not be worth as much as one good strong colony that would give you 200 or 300 pounds of honey.

Several years ago one of my sons bought nine colonies of bees in common box hives, about the first of June. He brought them home and transferred them at once to movable-frame hives, and in about three weeks divided them, making 20 colonies of the 9 he bought, using some queen-cells I had on hand for his surplus colonies. He then attended to those 20 colonies so they were all strong at the commencement of our buckwheat harvest. I then lent him 20 hives of empty combs to put on top of his colonies to extract from. He too 2849 lbs. of extracted honey from those 9 colonies and their increase, and left them in good condition so every one came out the next spring in fine order.

Another son, the same season, took one colony, divided into three, and received 347 lbs. of extracted honey. They also came through the following winter in good condition. I speak of these cases simply to show that it is not necessary to keep hundreds of colonies in order to get a little honey. If you will only keep strong colonies and give them the best of care you will soon find both pleasure and profit in bee-keeping.

Now in regard to the criticism on this way of making our increase. I find that nearly all who have made a failure of the method have taken colonies that had already made some preparations for swarming by having eggs or larvæ in their queen-cells.

I received a few letters from parties who had made a failure of this method in about the same way. Some had taken colonies that had capped queen-cells in their hives at the time they put the queen in the under hive, and, of course, they swarmed in a day or two. I can not see that these failures are any proof of fault in the method. When we work with our bees we must always use some discretion in such matters. If a colony is very strong in bees it certainly requires different management from one rather weak.

In conclusion I advise you to look over all the combs very carefully for eggs or larvæ in the queen-cells of the colonies you wish to divide. If you find any it is sure proof of their intention of swarming; then you had better leave them only a few days together. The number you must decide yourself according to the age of the eggs or larvæ in their queen-cells. If you are careful about this part I am sure you will find it a fine way to make a large increase, and at the same time have your colonies in good condition for any harvest.

April, 1906.

HOW TO DISPOSE OF NEW SWARMS AND THUS CONTROL UNDESIRABLE INCREASE.

While many are trying to invent some unnatural complicated hive, with the erroneous belief that it will prevent bees from desiring to swarm, and still others are recommending equally unnatural methods in spending valuable time in changing their brood from hive to hive all over the apiary, in hopes that they can overcome one of the strongest natural laws that the Creator has stamped indelibly on our bees, I for one will try to use the intelligence God has given me to work in harmony with his law, and see if, by so doing, we can not accomplish far more, and at the same time do it much easier, than to work continually in discord.

If, in the past, man had only let reason harmonize a little more with natural law the world would have been the better for it. There is one thing that I have noticed recently that I was sorry to see; that is, some go so far as to say that swarming is a *curse* to bee-keeping, and that it is a bane to our welfare.

Let us consider which of all the many theories and methods that are now before us is the practical one to care for a colony that has just swarmed, in order that they can all be united again, and at the same time do away with any desire to swarm again that season. From a long and extensive experience along this line we find the following method far better than any other that has ever been made public. It is this:

HOW TO MAKE THE SWARM CONTENTED.

We will suppose the colony is swarming, and we give them a hive which has its frames filled with foundation. This will give them a chance to use up the material for wax that is fast accumulating in their bodies; and after they are all in the new hive we will bring it back to the parent colony and set it on top, facing an opposite direction. This gives them a new location to work from, and is of much importance. Now leave them undisturbed until about night of the fourth day, then just before dark set the new swarm to one side out of the way and remove every comb from the old colony and shake the bees in the grass two or three feet from their hive, and be sure you remove every queen-cell from their combs and return them to the old hive; then shake the combs of the new swarm on top of the other bees in the grass; look up their queen and let her run into the old hive with some of her own bees. Now put on an excluder; and if you are running your bees for extracted honey set the hive of new drawn combs on top of the excluder, and the colony will all work in harmony together. If you are running your bees for comb honey, put on supers of sections filled with foundation. This will enable them to continue building comb, which has much to do with their becoming satisfied. Now as to why this method is a success: I will say it is all natural. First, the bees have been gratified in their desire to swarm; their queen has returned, during the four days she was in the new hive, to her normal condition of egg-laying; the bees have and are working off the accumulated wax that nature had given them, and they become satisfied with a new location; the old colony that had a lot of young queens maturing has lost them all, they hardly know how, and gladly welcome their mother home again, while the bees that constituted the swarm are so demoralized by losing their location that they soon form a line down one side of the hive to the old entrance. This gives us again a strong full colony ready to settle down to work; and, if properly cared for, they will gather more honey than under any other conditions. With us, not five per cent when treated as above show any desire to swarm again during the season. I will admit that he who is competent to care for only a few colonies may prevent swarming, and secure a fair surplus by this endless amount of tinkering with his brood; but it is unnatural, discouraging, and demoralizing to the bees, and, if practiced by our extensive honey-producers, would require so much help that, from a money point of view, it could not be otherwise than a flat failure.

I do not like to tear down the theories of any man without substituting something better in their place, which I am sure I have given in the above. Since we practiced this method we are pleased to see a colony swarm, and often wish that more of our bees would swarm than do, for we are sure to get our largest surplus from colonies that are treated as above described.

I don't think that there is any other condition a colony of bees can be in where they will work with such perseverance as when their desire to swarm has been gratified. Some of the nearest apiaries to us have swarmed a great deal this season, while we have had only 31 swarms all told up to Aug. 1, and this from an apiary of 750 colonies, and about 20 of these were caused by a blunder we made in June.

I speak of this small per cent of swarms during a decidedly swarming year to show that, while we allow our bees to carry out their natural instinct, we also apply natural methods to work in harmony with their desires, thus bringing two or more elements to work together, which has much to do with success.

August, 1906.

Since the above article was published, giving our way of treating undesirable increase, several letters of inquiry have been received as to how that method could be applied to colonies kept in a close house-apiary. Yesterday I received a letter from a friend, wishing some more light on this subject from me, for those who are keeping their bees, like himself, in close buildings. I can see no reason why this method would not be practical when applied to house-apiaries. All that will be necessary is to make a temporary stand for the new swarm as near as possible to the parent colony on the outside of the building, only have the new swarm face in the opposite direction, so that they will realize they have a new location. Then in four days remove all queen-cells from the parent colony and mix up the bees of the new swarm with those of the old colony as best you can, using some smoke so as to demoralize them as they are again united into one large colony. Then remove the temporary stand that the new swarm occupied, and the bees will soon locate anew in their old home.

I do hope every bee-keeper in the land, who does not care for increase, will give this method of treating undesirable swarms a thorough trial another season. With us it is the easiest way we have ever tried to keep down increase, and at the same time have all colonies strong in bees and maturing brood to make them still stronger in their working force; and certainly they will work with more perseverance, and give us more surplus, than when kept from swarming by removing queen-cells, which puts them in a sulking condition, wasting much of their time through our best harvests, which we should always try to avoid.

April, 1907.

TRANSFERRING BEES.

WHY IT IS BEST TO PLACE THE OLD HIVE BELOW THE NEW ONE.

Some have asked, referring to transferring, why I prefer putting the undesirable hive under the one I wish to keep the bees in, instead of on top, I will say I have always found them more inclined to commence work above their brood where the temperature is warmer and more even than under the excluder or near the entrance. I should have mentioned that it would be much better to place a frame of brood in the new hive, then the bees would go up, and the queen continue to lay. She will seldom commence laying in dry combs for several days, either above or below the excluder, unless the colony is strong and honey is coming in fast. One of the principal reasons for putting the old hive under is that, at the end of three weeks, it will contain but little honey, and its combs will be about ready for wax; whereas if the old hive is placed on top, then we have but little honey in the new hive, and the old one is full of honey in an undesirable condition. This is especially so if we use foundation instead of empty combs. It is for these reasons that I prefer putting the old hive under the new one.

In one case the new colony at the end of three weeks will be all that could be desired. In the other case the new colony would be light in honey, and, consequently, scant of brood, and its foundation very poorly drawn out. I do not put the new hive under the old one. The object to be gained is to draw all that is good in the old hive into the new one as soon as possible; and from our experience we find the above to be the better way.

March, 1908.

PART III

Honey Production

A FEW OF THE MANY THINGS TO TAKE INTO CONSIDERATION WHEN PRODUCING EXTRACTED HONEY.

In order to make the production of extracted honey profitable at the present time it is necessary to have every thing connected with the business as handy and convenient as it can possibly be made, and then try to cut corners here and there and everywhere you can.

First, it is very essential to have the best honey-gathering strain of bees that you can find; then if you expect to have a large apiary, location is an important factor.

Then the manner of handling your extracting-combs and taking them from the hive to the extractor is another important part; and the number of men who can work to the best advantage, so each one will bear about an equal part of the labor, and not have to wait for each other, is also of importance.

How to dispose of the honey after it is extracted is another thing that will pay you well to look after. The manner of storing it before it is put into the package you expect to sell it in must also be considered. These are a few of the necessary things that the successful producer of extracted honey has to keep fresh in his mind.

As I have received several letters during the past season requesting me to give the writers some advice on these subjects, I will endeavor, with the aid of the accompanying photos to show and describe our method of producing extracted honey.

HIVES SHOULD BE OF THE SAME SIZE.

First, we like to have all our hives of the same size, so that any frame will fit any hive in the apiary, although this season we had to press into service some hives that were two inches shorter than our standard hives, but we have promised ourselves that it is the last season that we will bother with two different-sized hives in the apiary.

HELP TO WORK TO THE BEST ADVANTAGE.

In regard to help, we find that three men can work to better advantage, and extract more honey per man in a day, than any other number. In order to accomplish this, one man stays in the extracting-building and does all the extracting; another man stays with the hives we are working at, and opens all of them and takes out about half of the combs and puts all the empty combs back and closes up the hive, while the third man takes out what heavy combs he can and takes the full ones to the extracting-building, and bring the empty combs back.

In this way we find no trouble in extracting from 30 to 32 hives per hour, or on an average a hive of nine combs in a little less than every two minutes. We always hang up a watch on the extracting-building so we can tell at a glance just how fast we are getting along. Each one, as he removes his comb from the hive, cleans it of all adhering bees, by first giving it several quick shakes up and down, being very careful to throw out no honey. Then with a small brush, what few bees are left on the comb are quickly brushed off. You will notice that, hanging from my son's right hip, is a small brush which we like the best for this purpose of any thing we have ever tried. You can also see the handle of a large pocket-knife by the brush, which is always open and ready for use.

THE ALEXANDER HEAD-RIGS.

I wish to call your attention to our head-rigs. They are made from a piece of common wire cloth, about 9x32 inches, with the ends lapped together at the back, and sewed. They have a piece of heavy sheeting in the back, which protects the back of the head, also our ears; then they have a piece of double cloth forming the top, and gathered at the center. They also have a little skirt about ten inches lond, which can be tucked inside the shirt or vest collar. With this on, so far as your head is concerned, you can bid defiance to all the bees in the apiary. Please make one of these head-rigs next season, for I am sure you will like it. They rest on your shoulders, and are very cool, seldom touch your face, and can be taken off and put on in an instant.

THE ALEXANDER COMB-CARRIERS.

They hold nine combs, the same as our hives, and are made of thin light pine except the ends, which are ⅞ stuff. They have an iron handle, and are very durable. When we commence to extract we take a set of empty combs in one of these carriers, and set it down behind of the carrier of empty combs, then put an empty carrier on top of it. This will bring it about level with the top of the hive, and saves stooping over in order to put the heavy combs in the carrier. Then when the hive is ready to receive its empty combs one man starts for the extractor with the heavy combs, while the other man puts the empty ones in the hive. In this way the hive is open only about 1½ minutes, in taking out its full combs and putting in a set of those that have been extracted.

NO SLAM-BANGS IN EXTRACTING.

Now, don't think there is any slam-bang about handling our bees, for there is not. We will not tolerate any thing of the kind. Any man who works for us must be careful about killing bees or jarring the hive any more than can be helped.

QUEEN-EXCLUDERS.

We use queen-excluders on all our hives when extracting, so we are not troubled with any brood in the upper hive; neither do we lose any queens if we shake some of the combs outside the hive. Our frames hang on a wooden rabbet, just even with the top of the hive; then we use an under cover, which has a bee-space on each side. This, with our telescope top, makes a cool water-tight cover which we like very much.

THE COLOR OF THE CLOTHING.

When working in the apiary we very decidedly prefer white. It does not irritate the bees as all dark colors will, and is nice and cool on hot days. I don't know of any thing that will make your bees much crosser than to work among them when wearing dark clothes. If you are careful about these things you will find it much pleasanter to handle your bees.

HOW TO STOP LEAKS IN HONEY-BARRELS.

If any of you are troubled with your honey-packages leaking, either barrels or tin pails, just rub the leaky place with common hard soap and see how nice and quick the trouble is over; also when barreling up your honey, after you insert the bung a little, tip the barrel over so as to bring the honey up solid over the bung, then you can drive it in tight and run no risk of splitting or breaking the head.

A GOOD HONEY-STRAINER.

This is one of the handiest and best strainers that was ever used for straining honey. A tin-smith can make them by cutting off the top of a stout tin pail 2 inches, then make a frame of folded strips of tin, soldering these strips to the top rim of the pail you cut off, then line the inside of this frame with the same fine copper wire cloth that is used for milk strainers, and you will have a strainer that will never clog or run over, as the honey can run through the sides all around as well as the bottom, and it will take out every particle of foreign matter from your honey, and with proper care will last a lifetime. I now have three that I had made over 25 years ago and they are apparently good for 25 years more. The way we use these strainers is this: Our honey-tanks are covered with sheeting, except about two feet at one end; this has a board on with a hole cut in the center that will let the strainer go down through as far as the rim that has the wire cloth fastened to. Then the pipe that conveys the honey to the tanks has an elbow on, that we turn down over the strainer. This conducting pipe is made in sections about 12 feet long of heavy tin, and has a bore of about 2 inches. We keep it painted on the outside to prevent rusting. Now when all is ready we start the extractor and our honey is delivered and strained into the tanks and we don't have to pay any attention to it whatever.

January, 1906.

I now wish to write a few lines direct to my brother competitors of extracted honey. The ever increasing demand for this product of our apiary is inducing many to turn their attention toward its production; and I hope to see you all so situated that you can produce it in the future cheaper than it has ever been in the past; for this reason, and this only, I write this article. If you have read the advertising columns during the past year in our bee-journals as you should, you must have noticed descriptions of an outfit for doing the most laborious part of producing extracted honey by gasoline power. Many people naturally hesitate in regard to investing their money in new implements, preferring to let (if I may be allowed to use some street slang) the other fellow invest his money first; then if it is all right they are ready to invest also. Now, my son and myself were just that other fellow that was ready to test this outfit to its very core. With three first-class extractors in perfect working order standing in our extracting-room we bought an improved eight-comb extractor and a gasoline-engine, to do our extracting.

Well, as to results, the first test we gave it was to extract about 3000 lbs. of last year's capped candied honey. The combs were mostly new and brittle, having been foundation last year, had never contained any brood; neither were they wired in their frames, as we have not a wired comb in our apiary. When the extractor was started and the comb-baskets began to hum like a buzz-saw, I at once knew that the old candied honey would have to leave the combs, which it did quite clean; but I expected that the combs and their frames would then and there dissolve partnership; but, not so. They were so well supported by the comb-baskets that we could not find a cracked or broken comb in the lot. The reversing of the reel is so perfect that you don't have to stop either engine or extractor in order to do this part. Taking it as a whole, it is certainly one of the most advanced steps in relieving us of laborious work ever made in modern bee-keeping.

Now the question is, in your mind, "Can I afford to buy this outfit?" Well, I will tell you what it is doing for us; then you can answer that question yourself. One year ago, with about the same number of colonies, we employed two men during the season, and a third man part of the time. Now we can do the work much better and easier with one man. You can figure out the amount here saved. During the extracting season we usually extract our combs six times, and we now find that such sets of combs, when taken from the extractor, are about 2 lbs. lighter than they have ever been before. Here we gain at least 10 lbs. per colony during the season. I leave this also for you to figure out—the many dollars' worth of honey saved on nearly 700 colonies.

Now, my friends, I think if you are running 100 colonies, or even less, for extracted honey, you can not afford to be without this outfit. The total expense to run the engine is less than 1½ cents per hour; and it is a willing laborer, always ready, and never tired. It can be used at any season to furnish power for running the cream-separator, churning, sawing wood, grinding bones for poultry, or any other work requiring one horse power. The directions sent with it are so plain that anybody can use it. Two men can carry it to any convenient place to work, and in a few minutes it can be leveled and ready to commence.

As I now recall to memory my first extractor, of some 37 years ago, which was a Peabody machine, the can as well as the combs revolved, and they had to be removed from the extractor and reversed by hand, the honey running out through the bottom into a small-sized milk-pan; and the waste and muss were dreadful. I can hardly realize the great improvements that have been made in honey-extractors.

Some time ago I called your attention to the importance of producing honey with comparatively small expense; but then the work was all done by hand. Now, when the most laborious part can be done with gasoline power, it reduces the cost of production to a still lower figure.

Why, I would as soon think of mowing a large farm with the old scythe as now to attempt to do our extracting with that poor right arm. No, that day is past and it will never return. We are surrounded with an element of progress, and every thing connected with the life of man is improving. The greatest achievements of the past are but milestones marking his progress to the sublime structures of to-day. There! I wish I could keep my mind on my subject.

Some may think that it is of little importance if one and a half or two pounds of honey is left in a set of extracting-combs, with a few colonies that are extracted only once or twice during the summer. I admit it is but little; but in our apiary it amounts to more than three tons in a season. This is saving enough in one summer to pay for several of these new outfits. You may think, "Well, if I don't get it all this time what is the difference? I shall get it the next time around." Yes, but you don't get it, and you never will get it. Under the excitement caused by disturbing them it is mostly eaten by the bees, and you are just that amount out; so I advise you to save every particle you can, every time you extract. It will all help to fill the barrels in the fall.

October, 1907.

HONEY-TANKS.

THE ADVANTAGE OF STRONG HEAVY CONSTRUCTION; HOW TO INTRODUCE LARGE NUMBERS OF QUEENS.

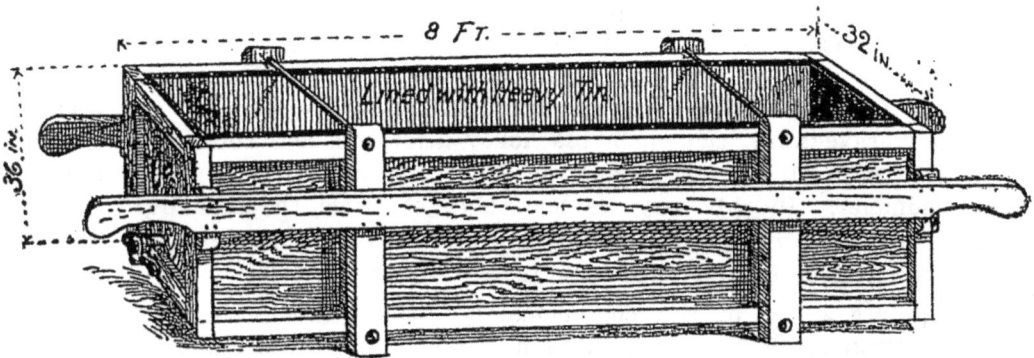

ONE OF ALEXANDER'S STORAGE AND EVAPORATING TANKS FOR EXTRACTED HONEY.

In answer to many recent inquiries as to the size and shape of our honey-tanks I will say that they are 8 feet long, 32 inches wide, and 36 inches deep, inside measure, and are made of ⅞ pine and hemlock lumber, the ends set inside of stout cleats. The bottom is cleated, also the sides. Here we have a piece of 2x4 joist bolted with ¾-inch rods from one piece of joist to the other, one rod across under the tank, the other on top.

We have one narrow strip of board on each side, which projects about 8 inches past the ends of the tanks, and forms handles to carry them by. This is very convenient. It is not necessary to make the sides or bottom tight. If there are cracks ½ inch wide it will do no harm, for the tanks are to be lined with the heaviest and best quality of tin that you can procure. Have the tin-smith put a large molasses-faucet at the bottom of one end to draw off your honey through; also see that every seam is well lapped and soldered or it will make a bad job if one commences to leak when full of honey.

After you have them empty in the fall, wash them out with hot water; and as soon as dry wipe them well with a cloth dampened with sweet oil. This will keep them from rusting, and, with other proper care, they will last a lifetime and remain as bright as new. A tank of the above size will hold about 5000 lbs. of extracted honey, and is the cheapest and most convenient article for storing honey in I have ever seen. I think ours cost about $16.00 apiece some 20 years ago. Make them stout in every way, for but few realize how 5000 lbs. of honey will make them bulge out unless made strong. You can make them any size you wish, but I wouldn't advise having them over 32 inches deep. Ours are 4 inches deeper than I wish they were.

June, 1906.

EXTRACTING UNCAPPED HONEY; A REMINISCENCE OF THE GOOD OLD DAYS OF FATHER QUINBY.

We extract our honey about every six or seven days when the harvest is good, never using more than one hive of empty combs on top to extract from; and, although this way of extracting is a perfect success with us, I can not recommend it to the inexperienced bee-keeper with none of the necessary appliances to ripen his honey artificially. But I do say that the man who has had experience, and has the necessary storage-tanks, can ripen his honey after the bees commence to cap it so that it will be just as good in every respect as if left with the bees all summer. In this way we not only get twice the amount, but we save our bees much labor and waste of honey in capping it over, and ourselves at least half the work in extracting.

Before a few of you commence to criticise this point I want you to understand that I never advised any man to extract and barrel up unripe honey, for, as sure as you do, you not only injure your own reputation but you do much harm to the whole bee-keeping fraternity; so, unless you have the proper place, and storage-tanks where it can be ripened as well as it should be, you had better leave it with the bees until fall.

I know I am one of a small minority on this particular way of producing extracted honey; but I would rather stand alone, and feel that I was in the right, than to be one of ten thousand and in the wrong. Please do not forget that we leave it with the bees until they commence to cap a few cells along the top of the combs. If the harvest is poor we sometimes leave it over two weeks before we extract, and run it into the tanks, where it always remains until it is good thick honey weighing fully 12 lbs. to the gallon. If I am not mistaken I think Editor Root sampled our honey in four different tanks last summer when he was here; also some that was in barrels ready for shipping, so I will leave him to tell you as to its quality.

When honey will granulate within three or four weeks after extracting, so it will not run through a large faucet, but has to be dug out of the tanks with a stout shovel in chunks like cheese, I don't see any need of letting it remain more than six or seven days with the bees.

Here is one question I should like to ask those who advocate letting their honey remain with the bees until it is nicely capped over. It is this: Will you please tell me where the profit comes in when you extract nice comb honey that is well capped, and can be sold for 10 to 12 cents per lb., then uncap it and run it through the extractor and sell the same honey for 6 or 7 cents per lb.?

If we could just reverse the prices of our honey I might see a profit in extracting nice comb honey; but as it is, and ever will be, to me it is the most foolish of all foolishness, and I doubt if any man in the United States can show and prove how he can enhance the price of extracted honey in the New York market, which handles more honey than all our other markets put together, a fourth of a cent a pound more than those large dealers can buy it for from other parts of the world.   It is all right for you to make all the handle you can over this point to your customers who take only a few pounds in a retail way; but when your product goes into the markets of the world in carload lots, then you will find that all this nonsense about leaving your honey with your bees until it is nicely capped over amounts to naught.   The dealers want honey of good flavor, thick and heavy, that, as soon as the weather gets cool, granulates solid, so if the head of a barrel should be knocked out it could be laid down and rolled across their storehouse the same as a box of cheese with the cover off.   Sell them honey of that kind and they will not care whether it was extracted every day or left with the bees until Christmas.

February, 1906.

FEEDING BACK EXTRACTED HONEY.

HOW THIS PLAN CAN BE MADE PROFITABLE IN THE PRODUCTION OF COMB HONEY;
THE IMPORTANCE OF THINNING THE HONEY AND FEEDING
DURING A NATURAL HONEY-FLOW.

My first experience along this line was something over 30 years ago.   The honey fed was thick extracted, and fed in its natural state after the August harvest was past.   This I fed for the purpose of finishing up partly filled sections.   I soon found this was a very unnatural time of the year for bees to build comb, as nearly every night was quite cold, with frequent frosts.   I also found that it took on an average a little more than 3 lbs. of extracted honey fed in this way to produce 1 lb. of comb honey, and it frequently granulated in the sections in a short time.

I next tried thinning the honey with boiling water to about the consistency of nectar.   This made a great difference in results.   The bees took it from their feeders more readily, and it did not require nearly as much honey to fill their sections, and I was not troubled any more with its granulating in the combs; but I was not satisfied to stop here when I could see that it required nearly 2 lbs. of extracted honey to produce one of comb, and I realized that I was fighting natural law in trying to force my bees to produce comb honey decidedly out of season.

My next step was to make extracted honey very thin with hot water, and feed it to certain colonies producing comb honey during the entire summer harvest, giving each colony about all it could handle during the night.   At first I was afraid it would have a tendency to check their work during the day; but, not so. It seemed to act as a stimulus to still greater activity when they could go to the flowers. Then I felt I had solved the problem of producing comb honey from extracted. There were no more partly filled sections to bother with; no more travel-stained sections to sell at a reduced price, but every one nicely filled out clear to the wood, and well capped.

I then found I had at my control for about 60 days as rich a harvest for the colonies I ran for comb honey as I could desire, and with not a break of even a day it was a pleasure to see those sections filled with choice comb honey.

I don't think it possible to feed thick extracted honey to bees for the purpose of producing comb honey so as to derive any profit from it after the honey-producing season is over. I think that nearly all those that have ever tried it, and went only so far along this line, have given it up in disgust. But when I took up this line of the business I went much further than any I had ever heard of, and made it a success.

The day is coming when the comb-honey producer will find it as I have stated above. He will have complete control of his harvest for comb honey simply by keeping a few more colonies and running them wholly for extracted honey to help his comb-honey colonies along during those natural changes of the atmosphere which frequently cause the flowers to stop secreting nectar several days at a time. Then the bees stop working in their sections, their combs turn yellow, and, if the honey-dearth lasts many days, as it sometimes does, it requires a good harvest to start them at work again in their sections, and then those sections will never sell for the highest market price. This can all be prevented when there is a good feeder under every hive, and tanks full of extracted honey.

I repeat that, in order to produce comb honey from extracted at any profit, it must be done during hot weather while the bees are gathering nectar from the flowers, and the honey, before it is fed, must be thinned with boiling water to about the consistency of nectar. To feed thick extracted honey out of season to produce comb honey is a waste of both time and honey; and the small amount of comb honey that is produced is likely to granulate and become unsalable.

This is one of those leading subjects which should receive our attention until our markets are free from so much unsalable honey as we often see. With the knowledge and appliances for producing honey we now have, no man is excusable for putting a poor article on the market; and it is a duty we owe to ourselves and each other to condemn this practice wherever we see it. I can not see how locality can make much difference in this matter; but I can readily see that, if honey is thinned to the consistency of nectar with boiling water, it will have a tendency to prevent its granulating; and if fed to bees in this condition during the season when it is natural for them to build comb and are gathering nectar from the flowers, a short slim harvest can be changed to a long rich one, for the bees will simply be helped to carry out their natural instinct, and success will be the result.

August, 1907.

PRODUCING COMB HONEY.

HOW TO RAISE A GREATER PROPORTION OF FANCY HONEY; A PLAN TO HOLD BACK
SWARMING AND AT THE SAME TIME KEEP WORK GOING IN
THE SUPER DURING A LULL IN THE HONEY-FLOW.

Although it is now about 20 years since I gave up this part of the bee business I often think I should like to call the attention of comb-honey producers to some important points connected with this branch of bee-keeping. The natural desire to swarm has always been a serious trouble in producing comb honey. Then the frequent change in our atmosphere, causing the flowers to stop secreting nectar sometimes for several days at a time during our otherwise best harvest is another serious trouble in producing comb honey of the finest quality; and with many the trouble of getting their sections all well filled at the close of the season is a hard problem to solve.

We will first consider the natural desire to swarm. This is the honey-bees' natural way to perpetuate their race, and is the most strongly imbeded law, not only of the whole animal world, but the vegetable world also, except the desire for food, of any law connected with our existence. This is why we have made *no progress* in changing the *nature* of our bees since man first tried to domesticate them. It is true that certain strains, or, more properly speaking, certain families, have far less desire to swarm than others. This same law can also be said to apply to other animals, including man. Now let us see what we can do to prevent the desire on the part of our bees to carry out this main object of their creation. First we will keep only bees that have but little natural desire to swarm; then we will raise their hives from their bottom-boards all around about ½ inch as soon as the weather begins to get warm. In this way we shall give them two or three entrances in the shade at all hours of the day. This, I know from experience, goes a long way to prevent the desire to swarm. Then we will supersede every queen at the commencement of our harvest, with one just fertilized, which, we all know, of itself will to quite an extent prevent the desire to swarm. Then we will see that their hives, including their clamps of sections, contain but a small amount of capped honey for any length of time.

Here is one thing that I used to be very particular about during my thirty years of producing comb honey: As fast as I could find four or five nicely finished sections in a clamp they were taken out and empty ones put in their place, never using more than two clamps at one time on a hive. I don't wonder that your bees swarm when two or three clamps of mostly capped sections on a hive and a lot of capped honey in the hive below, and then only one entrance where the sun can shiné down on the bees through the hottest hours of the day. This will make almost any colony restless, and frequently start a desire to swarm.

The honey-producer, until recently, has been justified in keeping his queens longer than one year, for it is only since Pratt gave us his method of rearing queens that we can have all we want early in the season with only a little trouble. If you will do as I have suggested in the above you will almost wholly prevent the desire to swarm.

Next we will consider the matter of a steady harvest, with no lost days, even if the flowers do fail to secrete nectar for several days at a time. This can easily be acquired in this way: First divide your apiary into two equal parts as to number of colonies, but have all your strongest colonies in one part and your weakest ones in another. Then run the weak colonies wholly for extracted honey and the stronger colonies for comb honey; and attach a good practicable feeder under every hive that is producing comb honey, and extract all you can from your weak colonies and feed it to those that are working in sections. Be sure to give them some *every night*. If the weather is fine, and they are getting considerable from the flowers, it will not be necessary to give them much; but if from any cause they fail to gather from the flowers, then feed enough to keep them busy in their sections night and day, with no stop until the harvest is over and every section is finished in fine shape.

Now don't say this can not be done, for I know it can. I used to produce comb honey in this way twenty-five years ago, and I am sure fifty colonies managed like this, with fifty more to furnish them with honey during bad weather, to work over into comb honey, will produce more first-class section honey than you could possibly obtain from the 100 colonies if they were all run for comb honey at the same time, as nearly all comb-honey producers do. The point is right here: In this way your comb-honey-producing colonies can have a *good steady harvest* from the day you put on your first clamp of sections until the last section is finished, and that is what counts, both in quantity and quality.

Nor, don't get this method mixed up with that of feeding back at the close of the harvest, but do the feeding when the harvest *is on* and every thing is in proper condition to produce comb honey. Make your extracted honey quite thin and give them one *grand big harvest*, and you will see your sections finished as if by magic. With two clamps of sections on, and a good young queen in the hive below, you need not be afraid of their storing too much in their breeding-combs. Then examine them often; and as fast as you can find five or six full sections in a clamp take them out; don't leave them to become soiled and travel-stained by the bees, in order that you may save yourself a little work, and take off a whole clamp at a time; for, as sure as you do, your bees are liable to sulk away their time and possibly fix for swarming.

It looks nice to go into your storehouse at the close of the season and see several tons of choice comb honey with hardly a section that is not of the finest quality; and to see the clamps all empty, with no partly filled sections lying around is another thing which shows there has been some skill used in producing that crop of honey.

Some of you may think that this implies lots of work, which I will admit, and so does every thing connected with the successful management of bees. I know many let them take care of themselves, and appear to be satisfied with whatever they can get; but I never should like to run a business in that way.

In the above I have called your attention to the three worst troubles in producing comb honey, and I have also given you a practical way of overcoming them.

About twenty-six years ago I sold nearly three tons of comb honey that was produced in this way to a dealer for two cents a pound above the market price, on account of its fine appearance. It is the same in producing comb honey that it is with extracted. You must adopt methods whereby you can combine a fine quality with a large quantity, and then you are on a straight road to success. If I should ever again return to the production of comb honey the above method is the one I should most *decidedly* adopt.

When I was running my bees for comb honey we had no practical feeders as we have now, whereby honey can easily be fed to our comb-honey-producing colonies; neither did we realize how easy it is to have an abundance of choice young queens early in the season to supersede our old queens with. Had I known then as I do now how easily these two important factors can be acquired I would not have changed from comb honey to extracted as I did; for I am sure there is more money in producing a choice grade of comb honey, as I have described, than there is in producing extracted honey.

May, 1906.

COMB VS. EXTRACTED HONEY.

COMB HONEY REQUIRES A RAPID HONEY-FLOW; MORE EXPENSIVE FIXTURES, MORE
LABOR TO PRODUCE; SWARMING CONTROLLED MORE EASILY IN
COLONIES RUN FOR EXTRACTED HONEY.

Frequently I receive letters from different parties wishing to know which is the more profitable to produce—comb or extracted honey. This, in some respects, is a rather hard question to answer, for much depends not only on the location and season, but also on the man and his methods. Rather than produce extracted honey as some do I should prefer comb honey.

There are many localities where the surplus is gathered so slowly, even in good seasons, that it is almost impossible to produce a nice quality of comb honey. Then there are many seasons, even in good locations, when the surplus comes so unevenly, by unfavorable conditions of the atmosphere, that this, too, to a great extent prevents the securing of nice comb honey. We all know that, the sooner the sections can be filled and well capped, then removed from the bees, the nicer will the honey appear.

Some years ago, in conversation with one of our principal honey-merchants, he called my attention to a fine lot of comb honey he had just received. Each section was glassed on each side, and the combs were as white as any new comb I ever saw. I don't think the sections could have been on the hive more than ten days. They were so white and free from travel-stains he told me he could sell that honey for 4 cents per lb. more than ordinary honey, on account of its fine appearance.

A location that will require the whole summer in order that a colony can secure 30 or 40 lbs. of comb honey should never be used to produce honey of that kind, for only a rich harvest with strong colonies and warm nights, so the bees will continue their work in the sections, night and day, will give us choice comb honey, and usually it is rather hard to have these requirements all at the same time; and if either is lacking, then we have a surplus of poor quality and a large number of unfinished sections.

Then there is the expense connected with comb honey, which we must consider. This is no small item in large apiaries. I hardly know just what it would be now, as it is a long time since I produced comb honey. But when I did, it cost me at least 2 cents per lb. for the necessary sections, comb foundation, glass, and crates. Then the freight charges were high, and frequently the honey got badly damaged in transit; and the worst of all was the uncertainty of securing much surplus. Then when I got the net returns from the commission men, and found they were only 10 or 12 cents per lb., with still another discount to be made of 2 cents per lb. or over for supplies, I gave up the production of comb honey in disgust.

The desire to swarm is hard to overcome in producing comb honey—much more so than with extracted. It is much handier to make increase, rear queens, or form nuclei in running an apiary for extracted honey, for I think these all require some brood when started, which never should be taken from a colony at work in sections, for it soon reduces their working force and causes them to be somewhat discouraged. This can be easily proven by removing their brood and putting in its place combs partly filled with honey.

Now, the question of labor is one we must consider. From our past experience we find, from the time sections, creates, comb foundation, separators, and glass are received from the manufacturer until the comb honey is sold, it has required far more labor than it would to produce a given amount of extracted honey. Whichever you produce, I consider it of as much importance to prepare your bees well in the spring for the summer harvest as it is to prepare them in the summer for the long cold winters of the North.

In the above I have briefly called your attention to a few of the many troubles in producing choice comb honey. With extracted honey it in many ways is so different that it is almost like another business. We have the whole spring season to rear young queens, make increase, and build them up into strong colonies; and although when the harvest comes there may be some still weak in bees, we know that they will give us some surplus, even though the season is a poor one, and the harvest is strung along all summer with only now and then a good honey day.

As soon as a colony is strong enough in bees, and is full of brood and honey, all that is necessary to do is to put on top a hive of empty combs with a queen-excluder between; and if you want them to commence storing honey above, at once exchange an empty comb from your upper hive for a comb of brood from below.

Some prefer shallow combs to extract from; others prefer combs of the same size as those below, and use one or two combs less in their extracting-supers. We prefer all combs in the apiary to be of the same size, and use the same number in the extracting-super as in the main hive. This gives more comb surface, so the honey will evaporate much faster than in thick combs.

Here is one of the principal reasons why we are never troubled with thin honey. A strong full colony that has plenty of room to spread out their honey and keep it hot night and day will thicken it very fast.

Storage-tanks are very important in producing extracted honey of fine quality. After it is strained into them there will be a little scum rise to the top, which can easily be skimmed off, and never should be allowed to go with the honey. Then it is easy to draw off the thick honey from the bottom, which gives you the very best quality that can be produced.

Comb honey is rather unfortunate in many ways. It is used only for table use, and here it has to compete with nearly all kinds of fruit, maple syrup, and a small per cent of extracted honey. But not so with extracted. There is a growing demand at nearly all times of the year for it. This is used mostly for manufacturing purposes.

As to the amount of comb or extracted honey that an apiary can be made to produce this is well worth considering. Some good bee-keepers estimate 2 lbs. of extracted for one of comb. We are sure we could never secure more than one-third as much comb as we do extracted, even though it cost far more labor.

Still another thing I like about producing extracted honey is that, as soon as the harvest is over, the work in the apiary is nearly done, except putting the bees in their winter quarters.

In the above I have tried to show both sides of the question to the best of my ability, and I leave you to answer your own question as to which is the more profitable to produce—comb or extracted honey.

July, 1907.

PART IV

Disposing of the Honey-crop

SELL EARLY; KEEP THE OLD CUSTOMERS; ADVERTISE; HOW TO UTILIZE THE HONEY IN CAPPINGS.

This is a very important part of our business—one which we should look at from several different points. First, we should take special care in producing either comb or extracted honey so that it will be of the very best quality; and we should put it up in the most convenient and salable package possible. Then we should have it ready for market as soon as the market is ready for it.

Here is a point that many are very negligent about. They have other work to attend to, and think their honey can wait until they can do their odd jobs, and foolishly they try to make themselves believe the price will rise, and they will get more later on. I have never known this to be so. On the contrary, the price is sure to decline until it is hard to sell at any price. Now, *don't* allow valuable time to slip by, leaving your honey on your hands, and then complain that there is no money in bees. Just watch a successful manufacturer or merchant and see how he is ever on the alert for any thing that can be turned to advantage; and if you expect to succeed as they do you must also watch these points.

In regard to sending your honey to commission men to sell for you, I must say that many times their returns are far from satisfactory. When you find a square commission man it is a very good way to dispose of your crop. But I pity you if you are caught as I have been by different parties. Before we commenced to sell our honey direct to dealers I thought seriously of going out of the business, as we could not produce extracted honey for the returns these men sometimes made. One lot in particular, of about four tons of as nice clover honey as I ever saw, he claimed to have sold at four cents per pound. Another lot of nearly a carload to another party brought us only three cents net, and I have good reasons for believing that each lot in question was sold for a good price. So from past experience my advice is to be careful where you send your honey. If you are a little short of customers, just advertise it in our bee journals and you will soon have chances to sell at a fair price; then you will know what you are to have, and when to expect it; and, as a general thing, you will be better satisfied with the result.

Another important part is, don't try to sell your honey for more than it is worth in the common markets. Here many make mistakes.

Some years ago we made this mistake, and lost a customer who had for several years bought quite a large amount. This time he paid us one-fourth cent per pound more for nearly five tons than he could get for it, losing about $25.00 thereby, where he expected to make that amount, and we lost a customer who at that time was worth nearly as much annually to us. If you can sell your crop in a small retail way I can see no reason why you should not have the same price as any other retailer. But when you sell in large quantities to parties who sell to those who have to retail it out in small packages, then remember that they must have a margin of profit to induce them to invest their money in it. This matter of holding a customer is well worth our consideration.

No man in business can afford to lose one if he can help it. Since we have given this part of our business especial attention we have had no trouble in selling our honey at a fair price early in the season. We think this a better way, and have the money soon on interest, than to hang on trying to squeeze out the last cent from a dealer who will never buy from you again if he can help it. I always like to have a pleased customer, for such are sure to buy another year. We have been censured many times by some honey-producers for selling our honey at the price we do; but I like to see the summer work all finished up before bad weather comes, and know that every thing is prepared for winter; then we can turn our attention to other matters for a few months.

During this winter season is a fine time to visit distant friends and make our plans for the coming summer. I think it does man good to have a rest from hard labor and mental anxiety. In natural law nearly every thing has a rest during part of the year except poor man, and he toils on until the worn-out body is lowered into the grave. But I will stop my sermonizing, and call your attention to another part of our business.

It is the caring for the cappings when extracting. I see many recommend rinsing them so as to save the honey that will not drain out, and then make this sweet water into vinegar. I used to try this plan, but I could never make a vinegar but that had an unpleasant odor and taste, and was nowhere when compared to cider vinegar. Then later we used to let the bees clean them up; but this had its bad features, and we were glad to adopt the following way of handling them: We now use an old honey-extractor with the baskets and reel taken out for an uncapping-can. We put in the bottom a screen of coarse open wire cloth for the honey to drain through, which keeps the cappings back while the honey goes out at the open faucet into the same pipe that conveys our honey from the extractor to the tanks. When this can is full we empty the cappings into a tight barrel and set them away until spring; then when we wish to feed our bees we turn boiling water on to these cappings until they are melted, and the wax rises to the top, which we remove, and then use the sweetened water to feed. Sometimes we add a little granulated sugar if we have used water rather freely, and it makes the finest feed to stimulate early breeding that we ever tried. In this way you save every bit of the honey from the cappings, with but very little trouble. I think if you will try this another season you will never again set out your cappings for your bees and your neighbors' bees to clean up, nor go to the trouble of making (to my mind) a very poor substitute for vinegar. I will admit that honey vinegar is sour enough, but I for one can not go that unpleasant taste.

Still another subject I wish to speak of is this: During those cold stormy days of winter, when time hangs heavy on your hands, and especially winter evenings, get out a lot of those old back numbers of bee-journals and look them over. You will be surprised to see how many good ideas you can pick up from them, especially the summer numbers that came when you were so hurried about your work that you hardly took the necessary time to read them, and still less time to remember and put those good points into practice. To sum it all up in a few words, don't waste any time in worrying about good or bad luck, but put yourself at the head of your business and realize that it is according to your skill and intellect that you either succeed or fail.

October, 1906.

SECURING CUSTOMERS.

According to what experience we have had in advertising our honey, there seems to be no trouble in disposing of a large surplus; and I am quite sure that a few dollars spent in this way will soon bring the producer and consumer or dealer together, and be a mutual benefit to each.

During the past three years we have sold honey in nearly every State east of the Mississippi River, and in a few States west of it. We have had some large orders from parties in Illinois and Minnesota. These customers we got by placing a small notice in the bee journals. If we would all try as hard to sell our honey as we do to produce it we should soon find a good market for the most of it. I hope to hear from others this winter on this subject, for surely we can not do anything of more importance to our business than to prepare ourselves for a large surplus before it comes, for come it will, and then we shall wish we had customers ready to take our whole crop. So, lose no time, but make it a point to secure some customers every season. The time has now come when we must advertise our produce in some way, if we expect to make a success of our business. I am sure I can see no other way to work off this surplus. Our village grocer can retail quite a quantity of extracted honey if we will furnish a keg to commence with. I know one party who sells nearly 1000 lbs. a season in a village of less than 600 inhabitants. He pays us 6½ cents, and sells for 10. His comb-honey sales are not as large nor as profitable as his sales of extracted honey. Give them a chance to make three or four cents a pound on what they can sell, and they will work off a lot of it. His customers bring a pail, and he weighs out whatever they wish. I have tried hard to produce and teach others how to produce large quantities of honey at a small expense; but one important thing in doing this is that you must have the best strain of bees that can be procured, and give them the best of care.

Now a few words in regard to getting good customers to buy your surplus. First, produce honey of the best quality—honey that is of good body and fine flavor; then through advertising in our bee journals let the public know what you have and its price. In this way we have been successful in procuring more customers than we can supply, and every season we have to return postal money orders and checks sent to us for honey after our crop is all sold. This season, about Oct. 10, soon after our honey was all gone we had an order from a party who has sold over 100 tons of our honey, for a carload to fill out a shipment to Europe. This order had to be canceled, and our only wish was that we had twice as many colonies of bees.

In conclusion I will say, deal honorably and squarely with your customers, so that, after they buy of you once, they will have confidence in what you say, and send their orders to you again in preference to a stranger. In this way you will find an outlet for your honey all over the United States.

December, 1906.

WHY IT PAYS TO ADVERTISE, AND TO GIVE AWAY SAMPLES.

I can think of no better way of getting our product before the public than to do as all successful business men do and manufacturers are now doing—that is, to advertise honey in every way we can think of. This is one thing we as honey producers have sadly neglected. If we expect to be successful in producing and selling large crops of honey, we must apply the same methods to our business that these successful business men do to theirs. Now as to the manner of advertising, each man must decide for himself. But advertise we must in some way. It is now high time we awoke to the necessity of this.

From the little experience I have had in having a small notice inserted in our bee journals and seeing its effect, I am sure that through them a nice large advertisement would be worth ten times its cost to any honey producer; and why so many of us, myself included, should be so negligent in this important part of our business is hard to understand. We know we have a good thing for sale—one of the best foods God ever gave to man; so let us join hands and place this before the public in a profitable way. Many business firms give away thousands of dollars' worth of sample packages in order to induce the public to buy their goods; and I sometimes think that if the honey producers of this country would give away a small per cent of their honey in sample packages for a year or two, it would go a long way toward bringing honey into general use. Then when the poorer classes get into the habit of using it on their bread in place of butter we would surely have a large demand for all we could produce. Most children are very fond of honey, and will nearly always prefer it to butter if they have a chance. This fact I often noticed in bringing up my family of four children. Here is a tender spot with many parents. They will buy for their children many things that they would hardly think of buying for themselves.

This is where the sample package would count big. The child would have some, then it surely would want more; and the indulgent parents would commence to buy, and they too would soon like it and buy often; but don't make your sample package too small. I would advise about a pound. Be sure to have it large enough to do for a meal or two. A mere taste would amount to nothing. Some may think to give away a pound of honey is rather expensive in order to induce a family to pur-chase some, so we will do a little figuring along this line.

We will suppose a man has 10,000 lbs. of extracted honey for sale. This at wholesale will bring him about $600. Now, if he gives away 1000 lbs. to as many families, and in so doing he finds 500 familes that commence to buy his honey at 10 cents, this shows his customers have cost him two pounds apiece or 12 cents each, and if they buy on an average 18 lbs. apiece during the season he comes out $300 ahead, or in other words, he receives $900 for the honey he would otherwise have sold for $600. This $300 would pay for all expenses of selling, and he would have a nice lot of customers to supply another year that had really cost him nothing. This is a case where it is necessary to sow before you can reap and like nearly all other cases you will reap accord-ing to what you have sown. So I repeat, don't be afraid to give away some honey in order to advertise your business.

There is one thing we should all bear in mind; and that is, when we get customers try hard to please them so as to supply them with whatever honey they may want year after year. No business man can afford to lose a customer if he can help it. First furnish a good article, then offer it at a fair price, and always be square in your dealings. If there is anything about your honey that is not as it should be, call the purchaser's attention to it. Don't wait until after it is sold, and then let him find it out as best he can. If you do, it is only natural that he will be a little careful about buying of you again. It might be of some help to have a circular go with each sample telling the value of honey for many purposes, and how the children were delighted to have it on their bread.

I sometimes think that we as honey-producers have never taken just the right course to bring our honey into general use. It is all right to teach the public as to its purity and healthfulness, but that is not enough. We must go still further and show them that they can save money by using it. When this is once accomplished we can then, and not until then, let this question rest. I have retailed in small lots but very little honey; but I have always noticed that, if rightly done, it is sure to bring good results. If we get a family to commence using honey they are sure to continue as long as we supply them with a good article at a moderate price. We have several customers who buy a 160 lb. keg of dark extracted honey every year for their own family use. They have got used to having it on their table, and they tell me they don't see how they could get along without it. They started by buying a ten-pound pail once a year. One man in particular bought six kegs this fall to retail out to his neighbors. This man never bought any honey until four years ago, when a friend of mine sold him a pailful. I speak of these incidents to show how easy it would be to start a large demand for our honey if each one went to work in the right way to bring it about.

Now in connection with the selling of honey let me say a few words in regard to producing. For some time there has been an almost unlimited demand for light extracted unless it is water-white and can compete with the water-white honey of California. This white honey is a hard thing for us to compete with and for this reason I would suggest that we try hard to have all our light honey put in sections, and sold as comb honey, and all our dark honey extracted. This would relieve the comb-honey market to quite an extent, and cause those who prefer dark honey, as many do, to buy dark extracted for their table use. I am often asked what our dark extracted honey is mostly used for. I find out from those who handle large quantities that the Jews are our best customers for this grade of honey. They not only eat a great deal, but use it extensively to make a certain drink which they like during their holidays. One of the largest dealers in New York told me last summer that these people used more dark extracted honey than all other classes put together. Then our large bakeries use considerably more dark extracted than they do light, and it is the same with all manufacturers who use honey. A very intelligent Jew once told me that their people were suspicious of all light honey, but had confidence in dark honey being what it claimed to be.

Personally we have been very fortunate in being able to sell all the honey we could produce, at a good price, as soon as it was ready for market; but I know that many others are not so fortunate, and it is for them that I hope some way will be devised so they may turn their surplus honey into ready money.

In attempting to write on this subject I fully realize that I am not competent to do justice to the question; but I hope you may find in the above some little thread that, when woven in with the knowledge of others, will be the means of bringing a better market to us all.

ORGANIZING FOR BETTER PRICES ON HONEY.

THE PRESENT UNSATISFACTORY METHOD OF PRODUCERS WORKING AGAINST EACH
OTHER IN THE DISPOSAL OF THEIR CROPS.

The weakest link in the whole complicated chain of modern bee-keeping at the present time is a lack of practical organization. I will admit that we have national, State, and county organizations, and we hold many conventions; but when it comes to the most vital part of our business, that of disposing of our honey, then each producer is not only a competitor against all others, but, according to his circumstances, will sell at almost any price he may be offered, thereby injuring the sale of other producers far more than ten times the amount he produces would if we were organized and sold at one price. This spoils the market, and the speculators take advantage of it and tell us and show us how cheap they can buy our honey, using the price and name of every party that has sold cheap, as a lever to bear down the price and enable them to buy our honey as they have many other lots.

It makes but little difference whether we count our colonies by the dozen or by the hundred, if, at the close of the summer, we sell our honey at cost. Then we are making no money from our bees, and there is something wrong. I know that, to organize for the purpose of securing better prices, would be a rather hard thing to accomplish. Still, I think something might be done to improve this part of our business. I have never known a season during the past 50 years of my bee-keeping life, when honey was sold at such a variety of prices, from ocean to ocean, as it has been during the summer and fall of 1906. Speculators have been scouring the country trying to engage honey at low prices. Many parties that had debts to pay sold at prices they would not care to have made public, while some, fearing that they would have their crop left on their hands, have also sold cheap. We see manufacturers, mechanics, and merchants all over the country organizing for self-protection, and it does seem to me that we as honey-producers might do a little in this line that would be a help to all. I am well aware that, when a man has debts crowding him he is in rather poor condition to argue with a speculator as to the price of his honey, which each party knows must soon be sold; but, fortunately, these are exceptional cases.

There is no doubt in my mind but that, if we could hold together as a company, we might secure one or two cents per lb. more than many do, and still sell at a reasonable price. This would mean thousands of dollars to those who sell cheap, and in doing so they spoil the market price for others. We, as producers, are too indifferent to this part of our business, and it is certainly high time that we awoke to the importance of this subject. If some of the valuable time that is usually spent over minor matters at our conventions could be spent on this subject it would be much better for us all. Now that the wintering problem is quite well solved, I know of nothing connected with bee-keeping of so much importance as that of organizing for the pur-pose of securing a more uniform price for our honey. So long as we continue to sell as we have done in the past for at almost any price that is offered, we are doing an injustice, not only to ourselves, but to all other producers. Like the drifting derelicts at sea, which cause loss and trouble wherever they go, so we, in disposing of our honey, sell for this and that price until we have spoiled the market and caused trouble to come to those who otherwise would be able to sell at a fair price.

For a long time I have been in hopes that this subject would receive special attention; but we don't seem to have any man who has the natural ability to organize us on this particular line. I have never taken any interest in organizing for the purpose of paying each other's lawsuits, for I never had a lawsuit in my life; neither do I take any interest in organizing for the purpose of getting supplies cheap, for I think the supply-dealer should have a fair profit on his business, especially the men who are spending both time and money in testing new methods, and are working with us to advance modern bee-keeping.

May, 1907.

PART V

Queens and Queen-rearing

SHOULD THE HONEY-PRODUCER REAR HIS QUEENS OR BUY THEM? USING EXTRA
CELLS FROM COLONIES THAT CAST SWARMS ONLY PERPET-
UATES THE SWARMING TENDENCY.

Frequently I am asked whether it pays a producer to rear his own
queens. This is a rather hard question to answer, for so much depends
on the ability of that producer, and on his experience in rearing good
queens. Many circumstances also have a bearing on the subject, such
as the number of queens required annually, the kind of honey produced, whether comb or extracted, the time the surplus is secured, and
the liability of the young queens mating with undesirable drones. All
these circumstances and many more should be well considered before
the producer decides to rear his queens. If he has but few colonies,
and is anxious to learn all he can about bee-keeping, without any regard to the amount of surplus he may secure, then I would advise him
to purchase a good breeding-queen and learn as soon as possible how
to rear choice queens. In that way his experience will be worth much
to him as long as he continues to keep bees.

One of the worst troubles in rearing a large number of choice early
queens here at the North is our cold backward spring weather. We
use about 400 young queens a year in our apiary, and have tried many
times to rear them during the latter part of May and fore part of June,
so as to have them laying about June 10; but it is almost impossible
to rear so many good queens at that season of the year. If we wait
till the latter part of June to rear them, then the bees from these
queens are of but little use as honey-gatherers until after the best of
the harvest is over. So we find it much better to pay considerable
money each year for our queens instead of trying to rear them.

About the first of December we gave a noted queen breeder our
order for 400 queens, to be sent us between the 1st and 20th of June
next. It requires time, bees, skill, and honey to rear good queens; and
when they can be bought for from $65 to $75 per hundred, and extracted honey is worth 7 and 8 cents per lb. by the carload, it does
not pay to sacrifice much surplus in order to rear queens.

When the ordinary honey-producer attempts to rear his queens he
is very apt to make some serious mistakes, partly through ignorance
and partly through a lack of time to give this part of his business the
close attention it requires.

If he would procure a good breeding-queen and rear all his queens
from her, then weed out and destroy all small inferior queens as soon

as they hatch, he might have choice queens without much expense except for a part of his time, and a certain per cent of his surplus. There is quite a difference of opinion as to the necessary amount of bees it requires to rear choice cells and queens. Some claim it can be done with but few bees; others want strong colonies to produce choice cells. I know we could never rear queens that would suit us unless we used so many bees in rearing our cells that it would make a sad inroad on our surplus honey.

The most common and the worst mistake that can be made in rearing queens is saving the natural cells and virgin queens from colonies that have cast natural swarms. I have heard this method recommended by men who were considered quite good authority, and it seemed as if I could not keep still and listen to them. We spend valuable time at our conventions in discussing various ways for preventing natural swarming, and we frequently see long articles in our journals from noted writers recommending certain methods to prevent it. Almost daily during the summer season we see bad results in our apiaries from excessive swarming, and then so many will do the very thing of all things that will perpetuate the desire to swarm, by saving cells and virgins from the colonies that are the first to swarm; and invariably when this objectionable method has been practiced a few years a strain of bees will be developed that is ready to swarm both in season and out of season. Nor is this all; for a great step backward is taken, and the bees from the first will begin to degenerate, and part of their yellow color will be lost; and the bees themselves being crosser and more irritable, they fail to gather as much surplus, and they become more nervous in winter. In a few years the apiary will have degenerated until it is of but little value. It must then be built up again with good stock.

In view of these facts do not take such a step backward as will bring only loss, trouble, and disappointment. When a colony has many valuable traits, send its queen to your queen-breeder, and write him, describing all those good points, and request him to rear the queens from her unless he may have a still better breeding-queen. In this way the choicest of queens may be reared from the best stock, and improvement can be made along the lines most desired.

As I look back I find that the seasons when we received our largest surplus have been, without a single exception, the ones following the year when we reared our queens from some special queen whose colony had given us an unusual amount of surplus the previous summer. It requires only four or five years of careful selection to make a great change in bees in their honey-gathering qualities, and in their disposition, until they seem like a different race of bees. The color is one of the quickest of all points to show improvement, and the tendency to swarm can be reduced to a surprising extent; but special care must be taken to select the best standard. Nor is this all. The drone-mothers must be just as choice as the queen-mothers. You must rear all drones from as choice queens as you rear your queens from. In other words, drones must be developed the same as the queens. This may seem like an unnecesssary amount of trouble; but there is little of value in this world that does not cost labor to acquire.

There are many bee-keepers who might make great improvements in their bees if they would only start in the right way. They seem to think that, if they buy a breeding-queen once in a year or two, it is about all that is necessary; and if her colony swarms they willl try to save some of the queen-cells, and then think they are improving their bees. Such a line of management is no improvement; and if that is the best that can be done, then it would be better to buy all the queens from some one who is doing better. The whole subject turns on this point: The best queens, bought or home-reared, are none too good, and the aim should be to make them still better with each succeeding generation.

February, 1908.

NUCLEI FOR REARING QUEENS.

Our nuclei have three combs each, size 5x9 inches, and about a pint of bees; they filled their combs so full that it was necessary to extract them frequently in order to give the young queens a chance to lay after they have become fertilized, and this was done some time before our August harvest.

Now, when little nuclei of less than one pint of bees can fill up their combs with honey in this way when there is no special harvest on, and that in an apiary of 750 strong colonies, it does seem to me that this fear of overstocking was only imaginary. A few years ago when we thought our bees went only a mile or so from home to gather nectar, we had some excuse for believing it was easy to overstock a location; but as it is now, when we have an abundance of good proof that our bees will work to a good advantage on flowers five or six miles from home, and sometimes still further, it changes the whole subject. Just think of the millions of honey-producing flowers, when the weather is favorable, within a circle of ten or twelve miles in diameter. This is the turning-point of the whole subject—"When the weather is faovrable." And when the weather is unfavorable for the secretion of nectar, it makes no difference how much bloom there is or how few colonies there are in the apiary.

In regard to these nuclei I spoke of above, we find them very useful. My son fixed up fifteen about the 1st of July, and by Sept. 10 we had taken out 63 choice laying queens from them to use in large colonies, besides some extracted honey, and the actual cost of these queens was not ten cents apiece.

We have tried many different sizes of combs for nuclei; but, all things considered, we prefer small combs, of which three will fill one of our standard frames; then when we put them in our nucleus-boxes we slide on a piece of folded tin so it makes a shoulder for the little frame to hang on. When we wish we can put a frame of these little frames in any standard hive, and have them filled with brood or honey; then the little frames can be put into weak nuclei if we wish, and at the close of the season these small combs with their bees, brood, and honey, can all be utilized in uniting with other colonies. I am sure that, if you will try this way of rearing surplus queens another season, you will be surprised to see how easy it is to have choice young queens on hand at a small expense, ever ready to use where occasion may require. If you expect to make a success of bee-keeping you must be on the watch to take advantage of all these little things.

December, 1906.

SUPERSEDING OUR OLD QUEENS.

DO NOT LET THE BEES DECIDE AS TO THE TIME FOR DOING THIS.

To supersede our queens when two years old, or to leave it for the bees to attend to, is a question of far more importance than many realize, and one upon which I very decidedly differ with some of our best bee-keepers. Last fall we had 107 queens in our apiary that were 2½ years old. Therefore for many years we have superseded all our queens at 2 years of age; but as a part of these queens were some we had bought, and were of an extra good strain, their hives being well filled with honey, and as some writers on the subject had claimed that the bees knew better than we when to supersede their queens, I thought I would test this matter thoroughly on a large scale, even if it cost me the 107 colonies to do so.

THE RESULT OF THE EXPERIMENT.

We put our bees in the cellar about the middle of November. These colonies, with their queens 2½ years old, were put in with the other colonies here and there all through the lot, and had exactly the same chance as those with younger queens. When we took them from the cellar about the middle of April we found only eleven that had superseded their queens; and it had been done so late in the fall that six were drone-layers, and the other five were about as weak in bees as those with the old queen; and of the remaining 96, 3 were fairly good, 26 were very weak in bees, and the other 67 were dead.

In looking over our bees about Sept. 1 we noticed that these old queens had all stopped laying, and had but little brood compared with the young queens. This fact, undoubtedly, had much to do with the weak condition of the few that survived the winter.

Of the other 603 colonies in the same cellar, that had queens 6 months old and 1½ years old, only 7 were lost.

Now, my friends, can any of you say that it does not pay to keep track of the age of your queens, and attend to superseding them yourself? I am sure it has always paid me well, heretofore, to do so, and I do hope that this costly experiment that I have just made will save many of you from a like experience. As I have written before, it is so easy to get the best of young queens now that have been reared from extra good honey-gathering strains that we have no excuse whatever for keeping old inferior queens in our apiary; and I want to ask those of you who advocate letting their bees do their own superseding if it would not have been *much* better for me to supersede those 107 queens last summer, at an expense of about $65, than to lose at *least* $400 worth of bees in leaving it for the bees themselves to attend to.

KEEPING TRACK OF THE AGE AND QUALITY OF THE QUEENS.

In the August issue of the *Review*, 1904, is published an article I wrote on keeping track of the age and quality of our queens, which is well worth more than a year's subscription to some of you who take that paper; and for the benefit of those who take GLEANINGS only I will copy a part of said article:

TIN TAGS FOR SHOWING AGE AND QUALITY OF QUEENS.

"Something like 30 years ago I cut out a lot of pieces of tin—some round, some half round, and some square, about one inch in diameter; and whenever I find a young queen commencing to lay I put one of these tags on the front of the hive on the left-hand corner, about two inches from the bottom. It is put on with a carpet-tack through the center, and is easily taken off with my knife; and it follows that queen to every hive she is ever put into. If she proves to be a choice queen the tag is put a few inches higher up on the corner of the hive; and if very choice, still higher. If she is inferior in any way it is put over toward the middle of the hive; if very poor it is put clear over to the other side. I use only one shape of tag each summer, with all the queens of that summer's rearing. The next summer I use another shape, perhaps round or square; then when I walk through the apiary I can tell at a glance the age and quality of every queen in the yard; and then when I have surplus queens on hand I can go right to the hives that contain my poorest queens and supersede them at once without having to open any hive unnecessarily. You see I can tell at any time. I see by the fronts of the hives just how many queens I have of a certain age, also their quality. If you will adopt this way of keeping track of your queens you will soon weed out the poor ones, and find it a great advantage to you to do so."

There, friends, I almost beg of you to take my advice in this matter, and adopt some simple method whereby you can tell at a glance the age and quality of every queen in your apiary. It is not only a source of much satisfaction to know the real merit of all your queens when working among them, but I assure you it is also, from a dollar point of view, one of much importance.

In regard to the proper time to supersede, I must differ with those who recommend superseding in the fall. My principal reason for doing so is this: If the queen to be superseded (as is generally the case) is old, and beginning to fail in keeping her hive well filled with brood, then you stand a big chance of having a weak colony the following spring unless you give them a young queen before August 1. In this section even our young queens lay but little after Sept. 1, and certainly we should have a good prolific queen in every hive at least one month before the breeding season closes. But if you are superseding good queens that have kept their hives well filled with brood to the end of the season (simply to get a better strain of bees) *then* you can supersede your queens almost any time during the fall; otherwise I should very decidedly prefer superseding all my queens early in the season.

Now, my friends, think this matter over well; and in doing so remember that your next year's surplus depends to a great extent on the quality of the queens you have in your hives this coming fall. The man who is careless in this matter will have many disappointments that he might otherwise avoid with but little trouble and expense.

July, 1905.

THE IMPORTANCE OF HAVING QUEENS REARED FROM THE BEST OF STOCK.

IMPROVING THE QUALITY OF YOUR BEES; THAT TWO-HUNDRED-DOLLAR ROOT QUEEN.

How many times during the last few years the different writers for our bee journals have told us the necessity of keeping young prolific queens in all our hives if we expect to get good returns! But how seldom have they told us of the importance of having those queens reared from the best honey-gathering strains of Italians that could possibly be found! This I consider one of the most essential things connected with successful bee-keeping.

First I will say that, of all the thousands of Italian queens that I have bought and reared since their first importation to this country, I have *never* sold a queen in my life, and I never expect to. We buy and rear only what queens we want for our own use; so hereafter, when I speak of the strain of bees we keep, or the strains of others, don't for one minute think that I am in any way interested in selling queens.

We now have what might be called a combination strain of bees, as they have been bred for nearly twenty years from the best honey-gathering strains of Italian bees that money could buy; and during this time I have thrown out every queen whose bees were poor honey-gatherers; cross or vicious in handling, addicted to excessive swarming, or were restless in winter quarters, wasting themselves away and coming out weak in the spring. All such colonies have been marked, and their queens superseded the following summer. In this way we have acquired as fine a strain of bees as there is in the United States.

You all know that, a few years ago, The A. I. Root Co. told us that they had found in one of their apiaries a queen whose bees gathered far more honey than any other colony, and that they saw such a decided difference in favor of this queen and her bees that they valued her at $200 for breeding purposes. Now, as I was fortunate enough to get 100 granddaughters of this $200 queen, and have had those 100 queens in our apiary for three seasons, I am sure I know something of their real value. First, we have had very few natural swarms from those queens—I don't think over 20 from the 100 colonies during the three summers; and when extracting we have always had very heavy combs from those bees, usually of nice light honey, even when our buckwheat was in full bloom. I am sure, therefore, that the blood we now have in our apiary, from that $200 red-clover queen, has given us several tons of additional surplus honey. I have also had some fine honey-gathering strains from other parties.

I wish now to speak of some queens I bought 16 years ago. I got 12 $1.00 queens from one of the principal queen-breeders at that time, which I introduced into good colonies about June 1. Although it was a good season I not only got no surplus from any of them, but had to give five of the twelve hives some heavy combs of honey from other colonies in order to carry them through the following winter. Twice since then I have bought Italian queens that were but very little better. Now, suppose our apiary had been stocked with such queens as those last spring. If so, instead of our having over 35 tons of honey for sale this fall, we should have had to buy several tons of sugar for feed.

How natural it would have been, if we had those miserable bees, to lay all the blame on the poor season or on the poor location; or, if some one had brought a few colonies of bees within five or six miles of the apiary, how some would have growled about the infringement on their territory, and the overstocked locality! Yes, my friends, too many of you have allowed your bees to degenerate into a miserable lot of hybrid mongrels that are not worth the room they occupy in the bee-yard.

Young Italian queens reared from the very best honey-gathering strains are now so cheap that I am very sure none of you can afford to take your chances on going through another season with poor stock. I will admit it takes some money and some work to requeen an apiary; but if rightly done it will pay you well, even the first summer. Then see what a fine yard you will have afterward.

In answering some of those other questions I will say, first, the season is of more importance than any other one thing; then the strain of bees; the management; and, after these, the location and some other less important matters.

My friends, there is no luck and chance in bee-keeping. If your bees don't give you any surplus, pry into every thing connected with them until you know the reason why. I can not understand how some men can be so indifferent to the most vital parts of their business.

Above all things, don't be discouraged when the losses come, as come they will; let them find you more determined than ever to push on until success and all its pleasures crown your years of labor.

February, 1905.

YELLOW VS. LEATHER COLORED ITALIANS.

A FEW WORDS IN FAVOR OF YELLOW ITALIANS; KEEPING THE BROOD-NEST CLEAR OF HONEY TO MAKE ROOM FOR BROOD.

For some time many honey-producers have shown a preference for the darker or leather-colored Italians. This would be all right if it were not that they have a tendency to degenerate back to hybrids and blacks when continued a few years. It is the same with bees as with all our domestic stock. We must have a standard to work for, and the color line seems to be very essential in our horses, cattle, swine, and poultry. Now, if we fail to keep up to well-marked Italian bees as a standard, then unprincipled queen-breeders can send us their hybrid mismated queens; and we, not having any fixed standard as to color, will have no chance to complain, as they can say they sent us queens of their dark Italian strain.

I for one have my doubts if any of the dark strains of Italians are superior to our three and four banded bees—that is, taking them as a whole in large apiaries there are occasionally some exceptions in each class; but one thing we must all admit; and that is, Italian bees are far ahead of our blacks or hybrids in gathering honey; but in order to acquire the best possible results we must give them in some respects especial attention. Their never satisfied desire to gather honey causes them to fill the brood-nest early in the season; but if this honey is frequently removed so as to give the queen a chance to fill and keep filled all the combs below the supers with maturing brood, then you will soon have a large working force, and you are then quite sure to get a nice surplus; but if you neglect to keep this honey out of the brood-nest, then you will have a weak colony and little or no surplus, which will cause you to become prejudiced against all yellow bees.

Next season make it your especial business to see every comb in all your colonies before you put on your supers. See that each one is full of brood from top to bottom and end to end; remember that each square inch of capped honey in those breeding combs costs you about 30 worker bees every 21 days.

The convenience and time saved in looking up twenty or more queens a day, as we frequently do during the summer season, is quite an item in favor of yellow bees. Some think these bees do not winter as well as the darker ones. I find that, where this is the case, it is caused by the Italian bees crowding the brood-nest with honey in August so as to stop all chance for breeding after Sept. 1; consequently they go into winter quarters rather weak in bees; and those they do have are mostly old and nearly used up. If you will remove two of the heaviest combs about Sept. 1, and put in the center of the hive two good empty breeding-combs the queen will fill them with brood, and your colony will be much stronger and better in the spring.

Still another thing in favor of our yellow bees which is of more importance than all other things combined is the fact that they are almost immune to that destructive disease known as American foul brood. Those of us living in this part of New York, who lost thousands of colonies a few years ago from the effects of that disease, now well how much we owe to those yellow Italian bees; for without .hem the production of honey in this part of the state would be a thing of the past. Sometimes I think the great loss we sustained was a blessing in disguise, for now we have better bee-keepers, better bees, and are securing far more surplus annually from our Italian bees than we ever procured from the black and hybrid colonies we used to keep.

When dividing or forming nuclei it is frequently quite difficult to keep the darker strains from returning to the old stand; but nut so with the golden Italians. I find that, if they have some brood, or a queen of any kind, they will stay wherever we put them. This is a good point, and often saves much trouble; then they will defend their hives from robber bees the best of any I have ever had.

Give these bees the special care they require and you will be surprised at the good surplus you will receive during poor seasons. Almost any bees will give us some surplus during a good season, but it is the well-bred bees that give a surplus every year. They will find nectar though they may have to go several miles for it.

Now don't think we have either bees or queens for sale, as we have not. I write the above only according to our experience in keeping bees of all shades of color from the genuine black to the yellowest Italian.

I might cite many more valuable traits that are well developed in those yellow bees, such as having but little desire to swarm, and breeding up fast in the spring. This is very much in their favor, as they keep their brood so compact that comparatively few bees are required to feed and keep it warm. Then it is easily proven that they cover a much larger field in search of nectar than the darker strains. I have often found them a mile or more further from home than the other bees.

With our well-bred Italian bees we now have good stock to work from; so let us unite in trying to improve them along the lines most necessary in developing a superior all-purpose strain of bees. This can be accomplished to a great extent in a short time; then bee-keeping will become more reliable, more profitable, and a much pleasanter occupation. It has been a long hard task to free it from the rut of ignorance and superstition of past ages; but we have at last placed it well forward among the intellectual pursuits of rural life; and now det us be careful and take no step backward that will check its forward progress along with other successful agricultural pursuits.

March, 1908.

REARING QUEENS FOR EARLY INCREASE.

HOW TO UTILIZE UPPER STORIES AND PERFORATED ZINC FOR GETTING SEVERAL
QUEENS FERTILIZED FROM ONE COLONY; A SCHEME FOR GETTING
A LARGE AMOUNT OF BROOD.

First, by way of explanation, I will say that in order to do this, we stimulate our bees by early feeding to early breeding, so we have many strong colonies quite early in the season; and in recommending this I am well aware that some very good bee-keepers prefer to have their colonies only of medium strength until about the commencement of their harvest for surplus.   But as we handle our bees quite differently in many ways from some, we try hard to have all the strong full colonies we can as early as possible, and we seldom keep a queen after she is two years old.   We supersede them some time during their third summer.   This necessitates killing about one-third every year.

Now, after taking them from their winter quarters we walk along in front of our hives and count how many we have that are two years old.   This is very easily done, for the little tin tag on the front of each hive tells us at a glance the age of the queen in the hive.   These colonies we now give especial attention to, we feed them regularly, and rather more at a time than we do the colonies that have younger queens. We also frequently give them frames of hatching brood from other colonies, and at all times try to keep them as warm as we can.   In this way we have no trouble in building them up strong and full of brood early in May; and while we are doing this we insert frames of comb that have some drone comb in near the middle of the two or three hives we wish to rear drones from to mate with our early queens. This should be done about ten days before we start the rearing of queen-cells.   Then about May 15 we borrow the bees from several of our strongest colonies for one day to start our queen-cells, as is now practiced by Mr. Pratt, of Swarthmore, Pa., which I consider the finest way to start the rearing of choice queens of any thing I have ever tried, as we have to use these bees only one day, then we can give them their queen and brood, which leaves them in about as good condition as they were in before they were disturbed.   When we counted up our old queens we found we had about 200 to be superseded.   Now, this will require 400 young queens if we divide each one; then we have about 100 colonies that have younger queens that we wish to divide. They will require 100 more, so we find that we shall need some 500 young queens to make our increase and supersede our old queens. Then we should allow about 50 for those that are lost, so we will start the rearing of about 600 cells.   We would much rather have more cells and queens than we can use than to be short only a few.   As soon as this is done we go to half the colonies that have two-year-old queens and kill their queens, *also* destroy any eggs or larvæ they may have in any queen-cells.   Then we go to the boxes that have our newly started cells in, and take out five or six cells for each colony that has been made queenless. These we insert near the center of their brood, and they will soon build them out into as nice cells as we ever saw. Then about two days before these cells are ready to hatch we kill the remaining old queens; then we tier up with two hives of combs all the queenless colonies we have. But be sure you divide the combs of brood and honey that are in the hive below about equal so each one of the three will have some brood and honey. Then insert one of these nearly ripe queen cells into each one of the hives as they stand on top of each other, and put a queen-excluder between each two hives; also have a separate entrance for each hive that the queen may use when she goes out to mate. You see, aside from the queen the colony has access to each one of the three hives through the excluders. In this way you will soon have three nice young laying queens in nearly every colony that contained your old queens. Then to use up our surplus queen-cells we form nuclei by taking one or two frames of honey or brood and about a quart of bees, and put them into an empty hive, and set them near the hive we take the brood and bees from so as to give them back to the old colony as soon as the young queen is mated. In this way we have no trouble in rearing and in having fertilized all the young queens we care for to make our increase and supersede all our old queens at the same time.

After you have practiced this method of rearing queens you will have no trouble in having all you want ready for use for early increase some time before there is any harvest of surplus honey in our Northern States.

With us this method of rearing early queens is so easy that we frequently have more than we can use. Sometimes we have 30 or more full colonies in our apiary that contain two or three laying queens each, nearly all summer, until we can find or make a place to use them. They make a fine colony to draw brood from. When there are two or three good queens in a three-story hive the bees all work from one entrance as one colony; for as soon as the young queens commence to lay we close up the entrance that was made for them to fly from, and they all work together.

Some of you may want to know what I would do if my queens were all young and I had none I cared to kill. In that case I would do the same with the colonies as in the case with the old queens, only I would save these younger queens in nuclei until I could use them in making increase.

We manipulate our bees so much through May and June that it is no uncommon thing for us to make 100 or more new colonies, mostly nuclei, to-day, for some special purpose, and then in a few days unite the most of them again with other colonies. We can do this very easily, as we use our common hives and combs for all this work.

I have made some assertions as to what might be made from 100 colonies in a year providing we gave them the best of care. I have received some letters that show the writers think I am in a tight place, and can not rear the necessary queens in time to make as early increase as I advise.   To those doubting Thomases I wish to say that we can rear *twice* as many queens as is necessary to double our colonies before June 10; and I assure you if you handled *your* bees as we sometimes handle ours, all that I have ever claimed *can be done.* Many bee-keepers seem to think that, if they set their bees out of the cellar about April 1, that is all there is to do until they hive some swarms and put on their clamps of empty sections. We find about as much to do from the time they are set out up to Aug. 1, when we commence to extract, as we do when we are extracting; and there is no slack time.   The bees are kept busy every day, either to rear queens, make increase, form nuclei, draw out foundation, or something that is necessary to be done by them in order to be in proper condition for our August harvest. We usually spend the last week in July uniting all weak colonies and nuclei with stronger swarms so as to have the yard well cleaned up of those that are not in condition to give us a good surplus. Then we can give all our attention to extracting and caring for our surplus honey.

In conclusion let me assure you that there is not much danger of having your colonies too strong in bees at any time if you will use them as you should, for they are the principal factor in making your business a success. We like them in the spring to rear those nice early queens from. We like them to make our increase from. We like them to get our surplus from. Yes, my friends, and there is a pleasure in putting away good strong full colonies in their winter quarters, as you would put money away in the bank to draw an income from in the future.

May, 1906.

DO WEAK COLONIES HAVE GOOD QUEENS?   WHEN TO REQUEEN; ATTITUDE OF FARMERS TOWARD BEES.

I have been asked to answer the following question: "After weak colonies are built up in the spring, according to your plan, do they usually do as well as other colonies, or should their queens be superseded?"

In answer I will say that I have never had occasion to supersede them oftener than other queens. With us all queens, when two years old, are superseded unless it should be a very choice one. We usually supersede queens for one of two reasons—either on account of their arriving at the age limit, or when we buy bees, as we sometimes do, they have queens of all ages and colors; then we supersede them as soon as possible, and in their place introduce good well-bred Italian queens.

I am often asked if it is not as well or better to buy our queens in the fall, at a reduced price, than to buy them in early summer. That depends wholly on the condition our colonies are in. If the old queen is failing to keep her hive well filled with brood without any apparent cause, then we supersede her in early summer; for if she is kept until fall the colony will have but little brood, will be weak in bees, and the young queen we give them will start so little brood that the chances are the colony will be dead in the spring, or so weak in bees that it will be almost worthless. But if the queens we wish to supersede are in full strong colonies, with their hives well filled with brood, then to buy queens in the fall for these colonies is all right; and if the new queen does not start much brood she will still have a good colony to winter in.

These are very important points that should never be overlooked in superseding our queens. I want a queen to occupy the hive she is to winter in at least 40 days before the breeding season closes. This gives her time to become acquainted with the colony and fill the brood-nest once or twice with brood. If we all look to this part of our business as we should we shall have fewer weak colonies in the spring, and in the end we shall have more surplus, and secure it with much less labor.

Another question I am frequently asked is, "What is the opinion of the farmers in your locality in regard to the effect of your bees working on their buckwheat-fields?"

Some 25 years ago, when we came to Delanson, it was almost the universal opinion that our bees would injure their buckwheat so as to make the crop almost worthless, but the farmers soon changed their ideas on the subject. The buckwheat here is all thrashed by men who have thrashing-machines, and go from farm to farm thrashing the grain for a stated price per bushel. These men soon noticed that, when they came within three or three and a half miles of our apiaries the yield of grain was much better than outside that circle; in fact, it yielded sometimes nearly twice the amount per acre. This was a surprise to some farmers. Their orchards also gave them much more fruit. The change of opinion among them has been so complete that they are now anxious to have our bees do well.

I sometimes wonder if there is any other business that has had to go through the mire of ignorance and superstition equal to bee-keeping.

Still another question I am often asked is, "Will the greater part of the honey in the future be produced by the specialist, or by men who have other lines of business to follow in connection with bee-keeping?"

In order to give this question any thing like a correct answer we must not only go back and review the bee-keeping of the past, but we must look upon it in the future as being subject to the same natural laws and conditions as all other lines of business. For some time we have seen a continual concentration of capital in every line of business. The men who have a thorough knowledge of their business, and an unlimited amount of capital, are fast driving the less fortunate out of business, and I can not see how bee-keeping can be an exception.

When I was a boy a large part of our farmers kept a few colonies; but now we seldom see any bees through the country except in large apiaries. And the same change will continue to go on until there will be comparatively few men engaged in the business, and these few will be located in the exceptionally good locations, keeping their thousands of colonies, and having the best of every thing connected with bee-keeping that money can buy; and they will sell their surplus at whole-sale to reliable parties, giving them three or four months' time if they wish, which often makes quite a difference in the price favoring the producer. There are many young men now starting in the business who will in time drop out; but some will continue, and they are the ones who will be the honey-producers of the future. They will first work for men having had a long experience until they have a practical knowledge of bee-keeping. Here, among other things, they will learn the value and necessity of a good location. To these they will naturally go, where, with their practical knowledge of the business, they can produce honey at half the cost that the inexperienced man can in an ordinary location.

May, 1908.

THE AGE OF DRONES; THE TWO-QUEEN SYSTEM.

In reference to the age of the drones, I will say that, in natural swarming, we usually find the drone comb of a hive well filled with brood capped, or about ready to cap, when the eggs are laid in the queen-cells. This would show that in nature the greater number of drones would hatch about the same time as the young queens or a few days sooner. For our early queens, then, we use eggs from our breed-ing-queen as soon as we find drone brood capped.

As to the number of our natural swarms, that depends much on the season, also on the length of time from one extracting to another. In our apiary about six per cent of the colonies cast natural swarms.

In regard to keeping two or more laying queens in a colony at the same time, and its effect on their swarming, according to our ex-perience so far, it has wholly prevented it, as we have never yet had a colony attempt to swarm that contained two or more laying queens where each had free access to all parts of the hive.

We are now wintering a colony with seven two-year-old queens in it, all loose in the cluster of bees. We saw and counted the queens a few days before putting our bees in the cellar; and up to date, Jan. 30, we have not found any dead queens under the cluster of that colony.

HOW LARGE NUMBERS OF QUEENS ARE INTRODUCED.

Another question I wish to answer, which many are inquiring about, is how we introduce the 300 or 400 queens every year which our system of management requires. This is one of the knottiest of questions, and one that has cost bee-keepers thousands of valuable queens. It has cost us so many that we now seldom try to introduce a queen into a full colony. We would much rather have our young queens hatch in what would be considered a small colony, and then as soon as she commences to lay build it up in two or three days into a good strong colony by giving them combs of hatching brood. In this way we never lose a queen, whereas by the introducing method many times the strange queen will be allowed to live only until she has laid eggs four or five days, and the bees begin to have plenty of larvæ to rear one from; then they will kill their queen and rear a young one in her place. We have lost hundreds of valuable queens in just this way, so for several years we have not introduced many queens into full colonies except when we have a surplus that we hardly know what to do with.

I think the day is not far distant when a large per cent of the queens that are bought from queen-breeders will be bought in a nucleus, and then built up into strong colonies by the purchaser. This is a fine way to make increase, and at the same time procure choice queens and avoid all loss and trouble in introducing. I think 100 good three-comb nuclei purchased in May, and properly cared for, will furnish enough extracted honey during the season to pay their first cost.

If not convenient to get your queens in a nucleus, then introduce them into small colonies that have no uncapped brood, especially if the queen is a valuable one.

I think queen-breeders are often wrongfully accused of sending out hybrid queens when the queen they sent was all right; but shortly after she commenced to lay she was superseded by a young one reared from her brood, which was mismated, and the purchaser never knew that the queen he bought was killed shortly after she commenced to lay.

June, 1906.

PLURALITY OF QUEENS IN ONE HIVE.

IS IT PRACTICAL TO HAVE TWO OR MORE IN ONE COLONY DURING THE SUMMER SEASON?

Yes, I think it is. With the ever pressing desire to increase our surplus we are anxiously looking for new methods whereby we can secure strong full colonies early in the season in order to take advantage of any flow of nectar that may come. This has caused us to do some experimenting along the line of keeping two or more laying queens in one colony. For several years we have known that laying queens will never sting each other if they can possibly get away from one another. This fact caused us to try some experiments along this line, with the following results:

First, a great increase in the amount of brood was noticed in these hives; in fact, they were so full of brood that but few cells were left for honey or pollen; and when extracting-combs were put on top a very large surplus was easily obtained. This fact alone was enough to encourage us in testing this method still further. Then another result from our experiments, so far as we have gone, is that we have never had a colony with two or more laying queens show any desire to swarm.

This is something we can not understand, as we expected these strong full colonies to be the first to swarm. In order to see if we could force one full colony last summer to swarm, we put 14 good laying queens into it at one time, and in about two weeks we examined it and found the 14 queens we had put in two weeks before, and their own queen all in harmony together, with nearly every cell in their combs containing brood; then during the rest of the season we used this colony as a queen-nursery. Sometimes we would take three or four queens from it to use in other colonies, and occasionally we put in five or six at a time, and none were ever balled or stung. In fact, there was no queen injured in any way in that hive during the season. I have seen three or four on the same side of a comb crawling among the bees, and whenever they would touch each other they would start quick in an opposite direction.

VIRGINS RECALCITRANT.

Now, don't think that you can handle virgin queens in this way, for you can not. They will sting each other or a laying queen as soon as they come together. There is not much you can do with virgin queens until they are fertilized and commence laying; then their desire to sting other queens is all gone. I have often kept two or three laying queens under a common drinking-glass on the work-bench for a number of days without their trying to sting each other.

The worst feature to overcome in giving our colonies two or more laying queens is in knowing how to introduce them safely.

Last summer my son Frank discovered the most practical method of introducing queens that I have ever heard of—a method whereby over 90 per cent are safely introduced and laying within 18 hours from the time the parent queen was removed. He wants to test this method still further another season before giving it to the readers of GLEAN-INGS; then if it still works as well as it has with us in the past there will be no trouble in giving our colonies as many laying queens as we may desire. If so, it will be another advance made in modern bee-keeping.

I can already see several advantages in keeping two or more queens in one colony. First, in requeening we would have to·remove only the oldest queen. Next, our hives would be kept very full of brood, which would give us strong colonies, and there would be no more complaint about our bees storing too much honey in the brood-nest. Then, for some unaccountable reason, it does seem to prevent the desire to swarm; and with colonies that contain nearly twice the usual working force we certainly would secure a much larger surplus. Our experiments so far along this line have been so encouraging that I expect to test it thoroughly another summer. I really enjoy testing and working out new methods, and I am thankful I have sons who can fill my place when I am gone. The young honey-producers of the future can not afford to remain long in the ruts we older men have made, but with renewed perseverance they must push forward until they have made great improvements over many methods now in use.

In the above I have given our experience so far as we have gone on this subject. Had my health last summer been so I could have tested this more thoroughly as to its bearing on natural swarming I should have done so; but as it was, I could do but little. To me it does not look reasonable that, to increase the number of queens in a hive, would in any way prevent the colony from a desire to swarm; but still it is barely possible that it may.

A particular friend of mine has been anxious for me to give our experience on this subject to the public, so that others could test it also this coming summer; otherwise I would not have written this article before another fall, for I have always made it a rule to write nothing but what I was perfectly sure was fact, and for that reason I desired to test this whole subject another summer before making it public. I expect this new method, in common with some others I have given, will be tried in a bungling way by a few bee-keepers so that there will be no possibility of its being a success in their hands. Then these parties will be the first to send in their reports condemning the whole thing. But, fortunately, this class is but small, and is daily growing less. This is encouraging; and when we all do the best we can we hope to leave the world the better for our having lived.

April, 1907.

PART VI

Wintering

LATE FALL FEEDING.

ITS ADVANTAGES; HOW 200 COLONIES WERE FED A SUFFICIENT AMOUNT OF
WARM SYRUP TO LAST THEM THROUGH THE WINTER; WHY
SUGAR SYRUP SHOULD BE SUBSTITUTED
FOR HONEY.

It is only a few years since the necessity of feeding bees in the fall was looked upon as the result of inexcusable negligence in the management. But time and experience are changing many methods, and we are fast learning that bee-keeping to-day is a very different business from that of years ago.

While visiting one of the most extensive honey-producers of New York, he told me that he and his father had for several years fed every one of the 1500 or 2000 colonies they had, just before putting them away for winter. They gave each one about 20 lbs. of sugar syrup without regard to the amount of honey the hives contained. This syrup was made from granulated sugar in the proportion of 2 lbs. of sugar to 1 of water. This was boiled until well dissolved, when about ¼ lb. of tartaric acid was added to every 100 lbs. of sugar. From their extensive experience in feeding tons of sugar to thousands of colonies they told me it was a much safer and a better winter food than any honey their bees had ever gathered.

The principal fault with all honey that I am acquainted with, except basswood, is that it contains some pollen that is carried into the honey-cups of the flowers by the wind or by insects, and then it is taken out with the nectar and becomes mixed with the honey, where it has a very injurious effect on the bees during the winter. This pollen is very noticeable in our large honey-tanks when they are nearly full of extracted honey, as it rises to the top, forming a scum sometimes two inches thick. This, when mixed with the winter stores, is quite likely to cause dysentery before the bees are taken from their winter quarters in the spring.

Now, with sugar syrup, since there is no foreign substance it is practically all digested, and the bees come from their winter quarters dry and clean, leaving no marks on the snow or their hives after their long confinement. This one advantage derived from sugar syrup, of itself alone, would far more than pay for the trouble of late fall feeding.

But there is another advantage gained by substituting sugar syrup in the place of honey. If it requires about 20 lbs. of honey to winter a colony, this additional surplus would be worth at wholesale about $1.50. Now, in its place, if we used 14 lbs. of sugar to make 21 lbs. of very thick syrup, costing about 75 cents, or half the amount the honey will bring, there is a saving of over $400 in an apiary of 600 colonies. Besides the bees are given a much safer an. better winter food.

We have been so well pleased with our experience along this line, and the experience of these noted bee-keepers, that we are now wintering some 200 colonies almost wholly on sugar syrup.

The first important part is a convenient feeder, one that will hold at one time all the feed necessary for one colony. This we made by taking 50 of our outside telescope caps, having a rim 2 inches deep all around. The inside of these we gave a good coating of hot paraffine wax, which prevents the syrup from penetrating into the wood, and also stops leaking. These caps are ¼ inch larger each way inside than the hive is outside.

We put a suitable float to prevent the bees from drowning in the warm syrup, and also put two cleats across inside the feeder for the hive to rest on; then about sundown we took these 50 cap feeders and set one properly leveled up near each hive we wanted to feed. With the syrup as hot as the bees could stand we poured into the feeder the amount we thought the colony required, then, carefully lifting the hive from its bottom-board, we set it inside the feeder directly over the warm syrup, and the job was done. The bees at once went down into the feeder and removed all the syrup long before morning; so the next day all we had to do was to set the hives back on their bottom-boards and place the 50 feeders ready to feed 50 more colonies the following night. After we had the syrup ready it required only about half an hour for my son and myself to feed 50 colonies. In four evenings, between sundown and dark, we had the 200 colonies all fed, and not a spoonful of syrup was wasted nor a handful of bees lost.

This feeding was done on quite cold frosty nights about Oct. 25.

Now, if we were feeding in early fall for the purpose of brood-rearing it would be necessary to feed much thinner syrup, and only two or three pounds a day, about the same as we would feed in the spring in order to stimulate brood-rearing.

Every year's experience convinces me more and more of the importance of feeding our bees at certain times of the year. We as honey-producers have sadly neglected this important part of our business.

There are many of us who neglect to do certain things both useful and necessary for the welfare of ourselves and bees, simply because we have no convenient and quick way to do the work. In feeding these 200 colonies I have just mentioned, if we had been obliged to feed them in our small spring feeders holding only about 2 lbs. each, we should have had an elephant on our hands; and the feeding, if done at all, would have required two weeks or more, as the bees would hardly have entered a small feeder so late in the season.

The principal advantage in late fall feeding is to have the bees store the syrup in and around the cluster where they have removed the honey during the last of their breeding in the fall; then this is first consumed by the bees during the winter; and by the time they commence to use their honey they are out of the cellar, and can frequently fly; so if their honey contains pollen, or is otherwise of poor quality, it can do them no harm.

I think the time is near at hand when the successful honey-producer will substitute sugar syrup for honey as a winter food wherever bees require a cellar for winter protection. In order to compete successfully with many that are now well established in the production of honey, it is necessary for us to be ever ready to take advantage of any thing that will add to our income, even though it may require the investing of some money at first.

We must certainly sow before we can expect to reap. This applies as truly to bee-keeping as to any other line of business.

January, 1908.

CELLAR WINTERING.

IS MOISTURE A DETRIMENT OR A BENEFIT? A CASE WHERE MANY COLONIES DIED BECAUSE OF A LACK OF MOISTURE; DISTURBANCE DETRIMENTAL; MID-WINTER FLIGHTS NOT ADVISED:

During the past few years there has been quite a change in the opinion of many bee-keepers on this particular point in wintering their bees. There is one thing, however, that we can all agree on; and that is, a wet cellar, with poor ventilation and a low temperature, is the worst place that bees can possibly be put in to winter; and some of us have found out, from long and costly experience, that a wet cellar, if properly ventilated, and kept at a temperature varying only from 44 to 48 degrees, is the best place that can possibly be made for perfect wintering.

With these dearly learned facts fresh in our minds, a year ago we built a model bee-cellar, 24x40 feet in size, which will give ample room for 1000 colonies, and at the same time give us a walk through the center from one end to the other. This is very handy in putting them in, in the fall, or taking them out in the spring; but its principal value is allowing a circulation of fresh air through the center of the cellar. We remove the bottom-boards from our hives, and set them directly over each other, with four one-inch blocks between the hives. They rest on racks 8 inches high from the floor, which is covered with about 3 inches of chaff or planer-shavings. This makes a nice covering to the floor, and enables us to walk among the hives without making any noise or jarring them in the least. It also prevents smashing any bees on the floor, which makes it much easier to clean up after they are taken out in the spring. The under course of hives rests on the cleats of a bottom-board turned wrong side up. This gives ten inches of space from the under part of the lower hive to the floor, which allows a fine chance for fresh air to circulate over the bottom of the whole cellar. You will also notice that, where we have left the under cover on, we raise it from the hive and put a piece of section under it, forming a little crack for the foul air in the hive to pass off. But we prefer a piece of light canvas over the top without the under cover on. In order to test this thoroughly, last winter we left some hives with both canvas and under cover on, as you will notice in the photo.

This cellar was built late last fall, and the walls were laid up with stone and Portland cement. It is 6½ feet between floors, and has about a foot of space under the floor, which is of matched lumber. Under this are two drains which convey water out all winter. The walls were very wet during the whole winter, as we had no time for them to dry, putting the bees in only one week after they were finished. Then in addition to these wet walls we put a building over it of green lumber, with a roof of galvanized iron. The floor over the cellar was of matched lumber, and double, with building paper between. This kept the cellar very warm with so many colonies in it; but with the perfect ventilation we gave it the bees came through the winter in as fine condition as I ever saw bees wintered, and only 2 hives out of 725 showed a spot of dysentery, although the bees were in the cellar from the 11th to the 14th of November until April 18th.

Last winter we had very changeable weather here. The temperature outdoors varied from 20 degrees below zero to 72 above—a variation of 92 degrees—while in the cellar it changed only from 44 degrees to 52, or a variation of 8 degrees. This 44-degree temperature inside lasted only about 24 hours, and was caused by a temperature of 20 below zero outside for two days, and the wind blowing a perfect gale. We kept a thermometer in the cellar, and could seldom find the temperature change more than one degree either way from 46.

In speaking of moisture in our cellar I often think of a bit of experience I had many years ago. I put 250 colonies in the driest cellar I ever saw. It was under a dwelling-house where two fires were kept burning nearly all the time. A short time after we put the bees in they became very uneasy, many leaving their hives and flying about the room. I had made a large tight room inside the cellar, of matched lumber, and put a plank floor in it. I kept the temperature about 45 degrees, but still the bees became more and more restless, and, when taken out in the spring, I shoveled up 14½ bushels of dead bees. That was the worst wintering I ever had, and it was a sight to see those that lived through the winter go to wet places after water as soon as they had a chance to fly. It seemed as if every bee went for water before it returned to its hive. Their honey was so dry and gummy that the bees could hardly eat it until it had been moistened with the water they got outside. The dead bees on the floor were so dry that, if you gave a handful a squeeze, they would crumble up almost as fine as corn meal.

Since my experience that winter I have changed my mind very much in regard to wintering bees in a dry cellar. The best success we have ever had was in cellars where there was running water, and the temperature kept at from 45 to 48 degrees. Many years ago, when father Quinby used to meet with us at our conventions, this wintering question was frequently brought up; and it was the opinion of us all at that time that, if a hive were made with double walls, and well protected on the top so the bees could keep the inside of their hive warm at all times, then they would winter well in a cellar at a temperature just above the freezing-point. But if we used single-walled hives with their bottom-boards removed, and on top had only a piece of cloth over the bees, then we must keep our cellars at from 45 to 48 degrees temperature, otherwise we might expect to have our bees somewhat affected with dysentery long before spring; and I am still of the opinion that the construction of the hives we use has much to do with the necessary temperature of our bee-cellars. Two very important requirements are perfect quiet and total darkness. These we can have much better in a cellar built in a side hill, expressly for our bees, than we can possibly have under our dwelling-houses. I think the amount of honey that is saved where bees are kept perfectly quiet will go a long way in three or four years toward paying the expense of building a special cellar.

Shortly after putting our bées away last fall I noticed a small bunch had gathered on top of one of the upper hives directly over the cluster. There was only a piece of canvas between the cluster in the hive and this little bunch on top. The canvas was well coated with propolis on the under side, and was tight all around, and had no holes in it so one bee could feed another, but still they lived without any thing to eat until the 10th of January, when I disturbed them so that they scattered themselves over the hive, and some crawled down and in at the bottom. I think there were about 30 bees in this little bunch, and I am sure they had nothing to eat for nearly two months unless their honey-sacs were full when they clustered on top. I speak of this incident to show that, if our bees can be kept at a proper temperature, and perfectly quiet, and so dark that the whole winter seems like one long night, it requires but little honey to take them through the time that they are confined in the cellar.

Now in regard to giving them a mid-winter flight, I am not at all in favor of it unless they are suffering with dysentery caused either by improper food or too low a temperature and bad ventilation. Several times I have set some out for a mid-winter flight on a nice day, but usually lost about all that were so treated. The principal trouble is that, after they are returned to the cellar, they never again quiet down and form a compact cluster as they do if not disturbed.

Last winter, about Feb. 1, we thought it best to put mats on about 200 colonies that had been left with the under covers on; and, although we had the floor covered with about three inches of chaff, as we always do to prevent any jar or noise when going into the cellar, and we handled them as carefully as possible with but little light, it disturbed these colonies so that they were quite uneasy for the rest of the winter, and wasted more than twice as much as the bees in the other hives did that were not disturbed. Another thing I wish to speak of in connection with wintering is this:

Many leave their bees out too late in the fall. Last fall we put 300 colonies in our new cellar, Nov. 11, and they had had no good chance to fly for over two weeks. The 12th of November was a warm bright day, and the 425 colonies left in the yard had a good flight all day. These we put into the cellar on the 14th; and when taken out in the spring they were in no way any better than those put in on the 11th, although they had had a fine flight some three weeks later than the others; so don't leave them out to waste away, as they always do with these cold nights of early winter. If we would all realize the importance of having our bees well prepared for winter early in the season, and then be careful and not disturb them any more than can possibly be prevented until they are carried out of their winter quarters in the spring, our winter and spring losses will be much smaller than they usually are.

When our bee-cellars can be ventilated in the proper way it is one of the most essential things connected with successful wintering. But when done as it frequently is, it is the ruination of thousands of colonies, being one of the principal causes of spring dwindling in its worst form.

January, 1907.

LOAF SUGAR FOR WINTER FEEDING.

QUEEN-CAGE CANDY NOT SUITABLE.

I once found 200 or 300 light colonies late in the season, with not more than enough honey for 30 or 40, then I resorted to all kinds of feeding imaginable. At one time I made a large amount of candy, from honey and sugar, and had very bad results. It melted and daubed up nearly 100 colonies so every one died.

Oh, dear! it makes me now feel bad to think of it; but I kept on trying one way and another until at last I struck what I still think is the easiest, quickest, and best way to feed light colonies, either late in the fall or mid-winter, of any way I have ever tried or heard of. It is this:

Make some rims two inches deep, and the size of your hive on top; then take off whatever covering you have over the tops of the frames of combs, and put on one of these rims. Then fill this rim with cut-loaf sugar—the kind that is in cubes about one inch square. Moisten this sugar by sprinkling a very little warm water on it, then cover the sugar with cloth mats so as to retain all the heat from the bees below, that you can, and the bees will soon come up into this rim of sugar, every one that can, and cluster in it and eat it as they require until spring. I have fed a great many colonies in this way, and never lost one. They usually come through the winter in fine condition, even though they had only two or three pounds of honey in their hives in the fall.

One winter I fed two barrels of sugar in this way, with good results.

Those of you who have light colonies to feed in cold weather, please try this method of feeding; and if you are as successful as we have always been you will never again try to make any candy for winter feeding.

We used to feed some sugar in this way after they were taken from the cellar in the spring, but we now prefer feeding a thin liquid syrup in our feeders for stimulating brood-rearing.

The colonies we have fed with loaf sugar as above described have always been in the cellar. It might not work quite as well outdoors in very cold weather. Still, if they were well covered up I think it would be a safe way to feed.

Feeding in any way in cold weather is rather poor bee-keeping; but it can be done as above stated, with but little trouble and seldom any loss.

March, 1907.

THE EFFECT OF DISTURBANCE; HOW TO MANAGE SO THAT THERE WILL BE BUT FEW DEAD BEES ON THE FLOOR.

It seems rather strange to me that any one should question the importance of perfect quiet in bee-cellars during the long cold months of the northern winters. I think our experiences must be taking diverging lines. For a long time I have thought that this subject of perfect quiet was one upon which we could all agree, but it seems there is a difference of opinion even here.

Now, before entering into an argument I will admit that there are certain times when the conditions are such that a disturbance among the bees is not in the least harmful. For instance, the disturbing influence of the sun on a warm balmy day in early November, even though it causes every bee in the colony to take a fly, can not be considered detrimental; but if on a cool cloudy day we open the hive with a snap and a jar, using smoke to enable us to replace the light combs with combs of honey, thus breaking up the winter cluster, causing the bees to fill themselves with honey, then certainly we have sown the seed of winter losses and spring dwindling. And, while it might not do our bees much harm to enter their cellar and quietly remove the dead bees from the floor, I do think it would be a great mistake to take off the bottom-boards and tops with a sudden jar, and then carry the hive-bodies to another part of the cellar, using smoke to keep the bees in, causing them to gorge themselves with honey. Then carefully sliding a dish holding a pound of warm honey under the cluster of a colony, and withdrawing from the cellar as soon as possible, might disturb them but little, as but comparatively few bees would be engaged in taking up the honey. But if you remove some of the center combs, and pour the honey into them, returning these wet combs to their hive, causing all the bees to fill themselves with honey, and to scatter through the hive, then again there would be cause for future restlessness and loss.

The injurious effects of disturbing bees in winter depends to a great extent upon how often and to what an extent it is practiced. When we wintered our bees in the cellar of our dwelling-house, with four rollicking children playing over them, it was no uncommon thing for many colonies to be badly affected with dysentery in February and March. Then it was "Hobson's choice" to leave them in the cellar and see them waste away and die, or set them out for a fly and have the most of them die after they were put back, for the bees never again quieted down into a compact cluster, but continued restless and uneasy until they were set out to stay.

In regard to the effect of a continued jarring noise over a cellar of bees, as in the the case of The A. I. Root Co.'s bee-cellar under the machine-shop, I would say that I have always believed this disturbance was very closely related to the necessity of so many mid-winter flights.

As to giving bees a sleighride of fifty or sixty miles in mid-winter, I am quite sure that there are not many that would care to have their bees handled in that way for much less than their actual value. I have brought home on a sleigh bees that I bought in the winter, and then put them into a cellar; but without a single exception I had to set them out early in the spring in order to save them. Bees handled in that way never will stand five months or more of confinement. I have never thought that it did any particular harm to enter a bee-cellar occasionally for a few minutes, if as little noise is made as possible.

But when from any cause a disturbance is made in winter to the extent that the cluster is broken up and the bees get frightened, filling themselves with honey, then because of the unnatural condition, they are injured very much and only a chance to fly will restore them to a normal state.

We have to-day, March 23, 750 colonies in our cellar, and the bees are so still with the thermometer at 45° that, when I entered this morning with a lamp, it was almost impossible to hear the least noise, and there seems to be less than 4 quarts of dead bees in the cellar, and not a spot of dysentery on any hive.

I have given many years of study to learn how to keep bees through a five-months' winter in that way, and I must say that, if there is any one thing connected with cellar wintering that has more to do with success than any other, aside from good food, it is perfect quiet. When we take a hive from the cellar with only about a pint of live bees, and see about four or five quarts of dead bees around it, we can hardly say that that colony lived through the winter; but when they can be placed on their summer stands after 160 days' confinement, apparently as strong as they were Nov. 1, then we can say we know something about wintering. This has been done, is being done, and can be done when they are kept quiet. But it will be a long time before it can be accomplished where they are subjected to harsh disturbance during long northern winters.   September, 1907.

VENTILATING OUR BEE-CELLARS.

There are but few things connected with the wintering of our bees that elicit such a difference of opinion as the ventilating of our bee-cellars. While it is true that bees have been and are frequently wintered in cellars that have little or no ventilation, it is also true that, in these, we usually find the combs badly molded, honey thin and watery, and the bees somewhat affected with dysentery, and far from a healthy condition when taken out. Certainly it is contrary to natural law to confine our bees under ground five months or more, compelling them to breathe the same air over and over thousands of times, and then expect them to remain in a healthy condition so as to stand the ever changeable weather of our spring season.

In constructing our building we had several objects in view. First, and one of the most important, was to give the cellar *proper ventilation;* next, to give us a large room above to do our extracting in, and store our surplus hives of extracting-combs and many other things connected with the business. Then we wanted a tank-room where we could have our honey-tanks so arranged that, in a moment, we could turn the honey directly from the extractor into either tank; then we wanted a shop where we could make hives and do all kinds of odd jobs, such as making beeswax into comb foundation, grafting larvæ for queen-cells, which should always be done in a warm room, and, lastly, plenty of room to store a large crop of honey in until sold.

First, I will describe the building, which is 24 feet wide and 56 feet long. The longest way is north and south. The cellar occupies 24x40 feet of the ground floor at the north end; then the tank-room occupies 16x24 feet of the south end, and its floor is on the same level with the cellar floor. This room has four doors in it—one wide door opening into the south end of the cellar; also one wide outside door in the south end of the building where we roll out the barrels of honey into the wagon when we ship. Then we have a door on each side of this room, which comes very handy to carry bees in and out of the cellar from the lower part of the bee-yard by putting screens on these two doors; and by leaving them open we get a fine current of air through the tank-room, which has much to do with ripening and thickening the honey. The cellar also has an outside door at the northeast corner, where the greater number of colonies are carried in and out. The shop part is on the upper floor, which is level with the floor of the extracting-room, and is 16x24 feet.

This extracting-room or store-room is 24x40 feet; and directly over the cellar in the floor of it we have four trap-doors about 10 feet apart, in size 2x2½ feet, directly over the bees. These we can easily open to any size of hole from a little crack to the whole space, 2x2½ feet, which allows all impure air to pass off into the large room above. We can also put a quilt in the place of the large door at the south end of the cellar, which gives fine ventilation into the tank-room and up the stairway into the shop, and up a garret. We have two pipe-holes in the chimney, one of which is always open, and makes a strong current of all foul air out of the building. This steady and gradual ventilation of the cellar into these two large rooms, one at the end and the other directly over the cellar, keeps the air as fresh and healthy where the bees are as it is outdoors.

With this way of ventilating the cellar it is never necessary to open any outside doors, letting in cool fresh air, which will arouse a whole cellar of bees to the extent that they never again become quiet, and form themselves into a nice compact cluster, as they should to go through the latter part of the winter without loss.

We were surprised last spring to see how few bees wasted away while they were confined in the cellar. The average loss was less than ½ pint to the colony, and that with a confinement of over five months. Every additional year's experience in wintering a large number of colonies convinces me more and more of the vital importance of giving them a pure healthy atmosphere during these long northern winters.

I often think that, if those who have gone to much expense building bee-cellars, and putting in ventilating-pipes conveying the air directly from outdoors in among their bees had only realized how much better it would have been to have had this air first tempered, as it were, by being a short time in an adjoining room, they would soon have changed their ideas in regard to ventilation. But here is the rock that shattered their faith in ventilation. When they saw this current of ever changing temperature from outside kept their bees restless and uneasy they went to the other extreme and closed up all ventilators in disgust, and have ever since been prejudiced against ventilating their bee-cellars.

This is one of the questions we bee-keepers have studied on for many years; and it does seem strange that it took us so long to see the great difference in results when our bees were ventilated by giving them fresh air directly from the outside or from adjoining rooms. The first has almost invariably done far more harm than good, while the second has given us the very best results we could possibly ask for, keeping our bees quiet and contented clear into the spring, so that it is not necessary to disturb them until the flowers are again ready for them to work on. I sometimes think how much easier it would be if we could look ahead and shun these hard problems of life; but then it is much better as it is, for it is through their study that our perseverance is developed, and in this way we are ever passing to a higher and a more intellectual plane.

With the continually changing weather of last winter it would have been almost impossible for us to prevent a very heavy loss of bees had we depended on opening outside doors to ventilate or cool off our cellar; for every time this is done it excites and disturbs every colony.

There are many things to take into consideration in order to winter our bees successfully. Many neglect putting their bees in proper condition as they should, early in the fall. I think this should be done before Oct. 1. Every colony should have a good queen not over fifteen months old; also a good sized colony of bees with at least 20 pounds of honey. This amount is sufficient if they are wintered in a good cellar, and you expect to do some feeding in the spring to stimulate early breeding, which is very essential in order to secure a surplus of early honey. But if you don't expect to feed any in the spring, then 30 pounds or more is better to carry them through to another season.

In the above I forgot to say that, during the winter, we close the inside blinds of all the windows in the room above the cellar, and the tank-room at the end. This makes these two rooms as dark as midnight, and with the trap-doors partially open, and the doorway into the tank-room covered with a light quilt, there is an even temperature of pure air at all times in the cellar, which keeps the bees as quiet as death, and with them it is like one long unchanging night from the day they are put away until they are carried out in the spring.

In conclusion, let me advise you by all means, when you build your bee-cellar, not to stop until you have a good substantial building over it—one that will extend either past the end or side of the cellar sufficient to hold a few thousand cubic feet of fresh air; then ventilate the cellar into these rooms, and you will have the whole wintering problem solved.   January, 1907.

PART VII

Bee Diseases

HOW TO RID YOUR APIARY OF BLACK OR EUROPEAN FOUL BROOD.

A CURE THAT IS EASILY AND CHEAPLY APPLIED WITHOUT THE DESTRUCTION OF COMBS, BEES, HIVES, OR UTENSILS.

This has been one of the hardest problems for me to solve that I have ever met in bee-keeping. For three years we tried every thing in the line of disinfectants that we could hear of, also putting our bees on foundation, which did but little good. Some of the things we tried seemed to help at first to check its deadly work; but in a short time it would show itself again as bad as before; and so the years went by while we lost nearly our entire honey crop and over a thousand colonies before we got the first sign of a cure, and even then it was so simple it seemed like a drowning man catching at straws. But I kept at the little proof I had until I developed it into a perfect cure. Then for three years we tested it thoroughly on hundreds of colonies, so that we could be sure it was a cure which could be depended on.

This cure is on the line of introducing new blood into the apiary, which will necessitate getting a choice Italian breeding-queen, one of the best honey-gathering strains that can be procured. For this special purpose I prefer quite yellow Italians. Now for the cure.

Go to every diseased colony you have and build it up either by giving frames of maturing brood or uniting two or more until you have them fairly strong. After this, go over every one and remove the queen; then in nine days go over them again, and be sure to destroy every maturing queen-cell, or virgin if any have hatched. Then go to your breeding-queen and take enough of her newly hatched larvæ to rear enough queen-cells from to supply each one of your diseased queenless colonies with a ripe queen-cell or virgin just hatched. These are to be introduced to your diseased colonies on the twentieth day after you have removed their old queen, *and not one hour sooner*, for upon this very point your whole success depends; for your young queen must not commence to lay until three or four days after the last of the old brood is hatched, or 27 days from the time you remove the old queen. If you are very careful about this matter of time between the last of the old brood hatching and the young queen commencing to lay, you will find the bees will clean out their breeding-combs for this young queen, so that she will fill them with as fine healthy brood as a hive ever contained. This I have seen in several hundred hives, and have never seen a cell of the disease in a hive after being treated as above described.

It is not necessary to remove any of the combs or honey from the diseased colony; neither is it necessary to disinfect any thing about the hive. Simply remove the old queen, and be sure the young queen does not commence to lay until three or four days after the old brood is all hatched. This treatment with young Italian queens is a perfect cure for black or European foul brood.

In regard to those old queens that were formerly in your old hives, I think it best to kill them when you first take them from their colonies—not that the queen is responsible for the disease, for I am sure she is not; but a young Italian queen that has been reared from a choice honey-gathering strain is worth so much more to you that I can not advise saving these old queens.

I have experimented along this line considerably, and found, after the colony has been without a queen 27 days, as above directed, it will usually be safe to give them one of these old queens, and the cure will be the same. Still, there have been exceptions, so I advise killing them at once.

Now a few words about your breeding-queen. Buy one of the very best you can for this purpose; for upon her real merits rests the true value of your apiary hereafter. I would buy a three-comb nucleus with this valuable queen, so as to run no risk in introducing her to a full colony.

Now, my friends, don't let another season pass without cleansing your apiary of this disease, and also at the same time requeen it with young Italian queens so you will not only harvest a fair crop of honey next summer, but will have an apiary that you will be proud of and take pleasure in showing to your friends. I know many of you have become discouraged in trying to rid your apiaries of this fatal disease; but that does not help matters any. The only proper thing to do when these troubles do come is to face them with a determination to overcome any and every obstacle that comes in your way; then when success rewards you for your perseverance, how pleasant it is to look back over the past and realize that you have accomplished all you labored for! I hope that you who have this disease in your apiaries will give this treatment a thorough trial next season.

November, 1905.

EUROPEAN VS. AMERICAN FOUL BROOD.

THE CURE GIVEN NEVER INTENDED FOR AMERICAN FOUL BROOD; THE BEES NOT
ABLE TO REMOVE LARVAE, DISEASED WITH AMERICAN FOUL
BROOD, FROM THE CELLS; THE TWO DIS-
EASES COMPARED.

I do wish I could impress on the minds of all bee-keepers that I have never recommended any cure for American foul brood, and I wish to have it nuderstood that I don't think that, up to the present time, there has ever been a comb that was affected by American foul brood cured of that disease. You might as soon expect a colony of bees to clean out their combs if filled with paint as to expect them to be able to remove the rotten larvæ from American foul-brood combs. I will admit that there are some things seemingly about the same in European foul brood and American foul brood, but in other respects they are no more alike than the mildest case of bowel trouble and the Asiatic cholera.

Many bee-keepers are continually speaking and writing of these two diseases as one and the same. Now, if it were not for the young and inexperienced bee-keeper I would not notice this mixing up of a very important matter. Then when my critics go still further and speak of the cure I recommended for European foul brood as failing to cure American foul brood, and in that way belittle that cure when I from the first wrote that I did not think it of any use for American foul brood, they do me injustice. You might as well expect to cure American foul brood by throwing a cup of cold water in the grass in front of your hives as to expect to cure it by requeening as I recommended for European foul brood.

The reason why American foul brood has never been cleaned out of a comb is because a larva that dies from that disease is so much like glue that the bees can not remove it in its soft state; and before it dries down it penetrates with its spores into the cocoons of the cell until it becomes a part of the comb itself, where it can not be reached by any disinfectants, nor removed by the bees. Such infected cell becomes ever afterward worthless to rear brood in. But not so with European foul brood. Even in its very worst stages, after the larva dies with this disease it soon dries up and cleaves from the cell, and is easily removed by the bees; consequently the cell is soon ready for another egg which often matures into a healthy bee.

Another point of difference is, a larva affected with American foul brood seldom dies until about old enough to be capped over, or after it is capped by the bees, while a larva dying from the effect of European foul brood seldom lives to be capped over, as it usually dies when from two to four days old. There is only one course of treatment for American foul brood, that is of any use. This is now known as the McEvoy treatment. That is, to remove the bees from their combs and put them on comb-foundation starters, and in two or three days remove them again to full frames of foundation. This treatment will save the bees, but is no cure for the combs, which are worthless except for wax. Fifteen years fighting this disease forty years ago, when this part of New York State was badly affected by it, gave me lots of experience. At that time I lost several hundred colonies with American foul brood, as we had no foundation then to use, and our only way was to cut out the combs as fast as it appeared and melt them up, and let the bees build new combs again. We cut the combs across just above the brood, leaving the honey in the hive with a strip of comb as a starter to build on. We did not then think the honey diseased, but I now know it was with American foul brood; but with European foul brood I have my doubts as to the honey being affected.

I have given many combs of honey from colonies badly diseased with European foul brood to healthy colonies, and have never seen a case where it had a bad effect. This fact, and that of the honey, combs, and pollen of a colony badly affected with European foul brood becoming perfectly healthy when requeened with a young virgin, as I recommended in my cure for European foul brood, is strong evidence that the honey is not the means of spreading this disease. It is very easy to cure an apiary of European foul brood; but the old American foul brood is incurable. As I said before, you can save the bees by the McEvoy treatment, but you can not save the combs.

I am well aware that on some points in the above I am crossing swords with those who are considered good authority; but on this subject in question I write the same as on other subjects, simply from long and extensive experience. I don't take any thing as fact until I have thoroughly tested it on at least 50 or 100 colonies for two or more years. This jumping at conclusions because some one says so and so, I think but very little of.

European foul brood will spread much faster through an apiary than American foul brood, and kill the brood quicker than any other disease that I ever dealt with. Coming as it does before the colonies become very strong in the spring, it soon reduces them to a mere handful of discouraged bees unable to accomplish any thing, and it is hard for their owner to realize that he will ever again have strong healthy colonies in those hives.

But don't be discouraged. I have been through it all, and what we have done you can do. All that is necessary is to follow the plan I recommended, and you will in a short time have as strong healthy colonies as you ever saw.

When we had this disease, black and hybrid bees were about the only ones affected. I sometimes think that, if the apiaries of some beekeepers were attacked with this disease it would be a blessing in disguise, for it would necessitate requeening their colonies at once with some good honey-gathering strain of Italian bees; and if this were done about the first of June these requeened colonies would be in a fine healthy condition for an August harvest; and then with a good working force of Italian bees their owner would secure a larger surplus than he could possibly have had if it were not for requeening to cure the disease. I think these black and hybrid bees cost us nearly all we can get from them, and what they lack in squaring accounts with honey they make up in stinging and boiling over and under their hives when one attempts to handle them.

February, 1907.

Addendum

PLURALITY OF QUEENS IN ONE HIVE NOT A SUCCESS.

Having had numerous inquiries from previous editions of this work concerning the plan mentioned on page 80 of this edition, for having more than one queen in a hive, we may say that, while Mr. Alexander, expert bee-keeper that he was, actually worked the scheme, we have since learned that not one bee-keeper in five hundred among the veterans is able to keep more than one queen in a hive after the honey-flow is over. It is quite a common occurrence to find mother and daughter in one hive at the same time. In that case the old queen is failing, and there seems to be a sort of "agreement" on the part of all parties concerned, bees and queens alike, that the old queen shall stay in the hive as long as she can do any egg-laying; but as the fall comes on, the old mother becomes conspicuous by her absence.

A few have been successful in working a plurality of queens in one colony at a time when conditions were just right. In the height of a heavy honey-flow, for example, the bees will tolerate a plurality of queens for a short time, or as long as honey is coming in freely; but in nearly all cases, as soon as the honey-flow stops all the queens will be missing but one. The fact that practically all of our best bee-keepers in the United States and Europe who have tried to work the plurality-queen system have failed, goes to show that the average beginner at least better not waste any time on it.

We have also had a good many calls for Mr. Alexander's son's method for introducing several queens to a colony. Mr. A., shortly before his death, described in Gleanings, page 1136 for 1907, the method as follows:

First, prepare a small box, about five or six inches square, by boring a half-inch hole in one end. This you will for the present close, then remove a part of its two sides and cover with wire cloth so as to ventilate it well. This we call our introducing-box. Take this box and a common queen-cage to the colony to which you wish to introduce your choice queen, or several of them, in fact; remove its combs and put its queen, without any bees, into the queen-cage you have. While doing this shake about a pint of bees of the colony into the introducing-box. Close it and take all their combs from the colony. These can be placed on top of almost any hive until next day. The hive now made broodless, fill about half full of combs containing some honey but no brood. Leave the colony alone until about sundown, after which it will show distress over the loss of its queen and brood. Now take the box of bees to the honey-house, and at the same time the queen, but don't set them near each other. The bees in the little box will soon miss their queen and have lots of trouble.

After they have been confined about five hours prepare some warm thin honey, placing it in a dish so that, by laying the box on one side, the bees can easily reach the honey through the wire cloth, but can not daub themselves with it. Leave them this way until you are sure that every bee in the box is as full of honey as it can be, then give them a little shake and remove the cover from the hole in the end of the box (remember it is about five hours since they were confined in the box), and let run in any number of queens you wish, including their own mother. Now return them to their dish of honey so they can help themselves to all they can eat until about sundown; then take this introducing-box with its bees and queens to the hive from which you took the bees and their queen in the morning; set them to one side and feed the colony all you can induce it to eat. Remove some of its combs and pour in some of the honey you have been feeding to the bees in the box. Shake some of this honey out of its combs on these bees, so every one will soon be full. Now remove the cover of the introducing-box and set the box in the hive alongside the combs. Close up the top of the hive, and in the morning all the bees and queens will be clustered on the combs, and some of the queens will have commenced to lay. You can now give them the brood you took away from them the day before, or let them fill their combs with eggs, which five queens will do in three or four days. That is all there is of it.

Now why is this method a success? First, because the bees have been a few hours without their queen and brood; next, a small part of their colony was confined in a box and filled with honey for several hours before the strange queens were given them; then those bees and these queens were shut up long enough together to become all of the same odor before they were given to the colony.

There are some things in this method that must not be overlooked. You first confine enough bees in the introducing-box to give to the queens you introduce the same scent as the colony is, to which you intend to put them; then the whole colony has been queenless and broodless for a few hours, and you have fed them in the box all they could hold before giving them these queens, and you have also fed the colony all they could eat before they received the queens and their bees. I find bees, like men, are better-natured when their stomachs are full.

BOOKS ON BEE-KEEPING

The bee-keeper who would be down-to-date and progressive will find in a recount of the experiences of others the very suggestions he needs for saving time and money. Very few other occupations have been blest with so many well written books covering the pursuit in its many different phases. To bee-keepers are offered authoritative works at a minimum of expense and the opportunity to gain knowledge in this satisfying way should not be neglected.

For the benefit of those who wish to purchase other books on bee-keeping—covering the subject in a general way or some phase of the work in particular—we have compiled the following list. These books may be had at the prices named from THE A. I. ROOT CO., Medina, Ohio, the publishers of the volume in which this announcement appears, or from dealers in bee-keepers' supplies everywhere.

THE A B C AND X Y Z OF BEE CULTURE

A. I. and E. R. Root. The latest edition of this work is the most complete of any bee-book that has ever been issued in the English language. While it is for the beginner, it may be read with profit by the advanced bee-keeper. Its sale is so large that neither time nor money are spared to keep this book fully abreast with the times. In the latest edition some scientific and technical matter as well as the practical has been added to its pages. It has been most carefully edited and revised. Its authors and publissers feel that, more than ever, it is a safe and reliable guide to bee-keeping. Nearly 130,000 copies in the English language alone have been sold. It has been translated into French and German.

In this edition there is a large number of half-tone reproductions from what might be called moving-pictures, showing various steps in the processes for handling bees. While a detailed description goes with the separate views showing each step, yet one can almost learn how to handle bees by simply looking at the series of photographs. Under the head of "Frames, to Manipulate," for example, there are a large number of new engravings that show not only the method of handling frames but handling hives and bees in such a way as to do the work with the greatest economy of labor, with few or no stings, and with but little fatigue.

The new methods of queen-rearing have been carefully reviewed, and the main points incorporated in the new edition, so that the practical bee-keeper who possesses a copy will have the best ideas of the subject constantly by his side for reference.

The new methods of wax-production are treated in an exhaustive fashion; and as this subject is now of more importance than formerly, more space has been devoted to it.

The new power-driven automatic extractors are amply illustrated and described. The subject of diseases has received entirely new treatment to keep pace with new discoveries of the last few years. The laws relating to bees have for the first time received full treatment. No other bee-book treats of this very important subject. The divisible-brood-chamber hive and the subject of swarm control have received special attention. Honey, sugar, nectar, and glucose, written up by a United States government chemist, are carefully defined in accordance with the demands of our new pure-food laws.

bee-keeping. Cloth bound, 270 pages, by mail, $1.00; by freight or express, 10 cts. less.

ADVANCED BEE CULTURE. By W. Z. Hutchinson; Revised Edition. This is a very unusual work—we might say indispensable to any one who is thinking seriously of becoming a specialist in apiculture. The author himself has been a specialist and right down to the present time he is in closest touch with these methods; and nothing now in print could be of more benefit to the practical bee-keeper than this book. It is fully illustrated, well printed, and is sure to please. Price by mail, $1.00; 10 cts. less by freight or express.

HOW TO KEEP BEES. By Anna Botsford Comstock. This is a charmingly written manual for amateurs, describing in the clearest language all necessary details. The authoress combines enthusiasm, literary ability, and a knowledge of bee-keeping into a goodly volume. Having herself made a start in the bee-business, she fully appreciates the perplexities of the situation and makes provision accordingly. The book is well suited to the wants of the suburbanite who wishes a hobby which will give something by way of return for labor and capital expended, or those who wish to keep only a small apiary either for pleasure or profit. If there is any better book than this for the purpose indicated, we do not know of it. Cloth bound, 228 pages, $1.00 postpaid; by freight or express, 10 cts. less.

BIGGLE BEE-BOOK. This is a very neat cloth-bound book, well printed and illustrated. It is 5½ by 4 inches, by ⅜ inch thick—just right to carry in the pocket. It is just the thing for the busy man who would like to get a birdseye view of bee-keeping, and who has not the time to read the more comprehensive works. The book is boiled down, containing only the best practices known. Price by mail, 50 cts.; 5 cents less if sent by freight or express.

A MODERN BEE-FARM. By Simmins, is one of those books which will cause you to sit up and take notice if you are a real live bee-keeper with lots of formic acid in your blood. The author is an English bee-keeper of note, who not only knows and understands bee culture in his own home land, but is as well an earnest student of American apicultural methods. He is not very orthodox in his views, but his book is all the better for that, seeing he wants to take us out of the ruts. You can read the book right straight through as it runs along like a narrative or a novel. Cloth bound, 430 pages, 1904; price $2.00 postpaid; by freight or express, 15 cts. less.

BRITISH BEE-KEEPERS' GUIDE BOOK. By T. W. Cowan. This is the leading English work on practical bee-keeping in England, and as such has had an immense sale. The work is condensed into 179 pages, handsomely bound and well illustrated. Price $1.00 by mail; by freight or express, 5 cts. less.

THE IRISH BEE-GUIDE, by Digges, is, as its name implies, a guide to the bee-keeping industry of Ireland. This is a closely printed, well-bound book of 220 pages with excellent illustrations on fine paper. It would be useful to any one who wishes to become acquainted with the status of bee-keeping in the old land. Price $1.00 postpaid; by freight or express, 5 cts. less.

THE HONEY BEE. By T. W. Cowan. A complete scientific treatise on the honey bee, its natural history, anatomy and physiology, by one of the foremost writers on apiculture. More than 200 pages—nearly 150 illustrations. Bound in substantial cloth, $1.00 postpaid.

WAX-CRAFT. By Thomas William Cowan. No bee-keeper of any pretensions can afford to be without one book on beeswax. This is the only book on the subject in English. Price by mail, $1.00; by freight or express, 5 cts. less.

These books may be obtained from the publishers of this volume or from dealers in bee-keepers' supplies everywhere.

POPULAR WORKS ON BEE CULTURE

The following books are for the most part by writers of well-known literary ability, and are very interesting indeed, and are greatly valued by bee-keepers and others for their literary merit, and the popular style in which bee-keeping is depicted, and we are very glad to have the opportunity to offer them to bee-keepers and others. The description of each work will give a fair idea of the same, but a pamphlet giving an extended view of these and the practical books on bee culture listed in the preceding columns will be sent on application.

THE CHILDREN'S STORY OF THE BEE. By S. L. Bensusan, London. This volume was written for children, and the author endeavors to tell the story of the bee before a youthful audience as completely as possible under the circumstances. It traces the life of the drones, queen and worker from the egg to the final destiny of each, telling the story of each in a semi-fanciful, entertaining way. At the same time, the book gives a very clear idea of its life, and will appeal strongly to all who know but little about these interesting insects. It has 250 pages. Price $2.00; 10 cts. less by freight or express.

THE HONEY-MAKERS. By Miss Margaret W. Morley. This is the story of the life of the bee, told in very interesting style—how it lives, gathers honey, and all about it. While clothing the general subject with an air of poetry, it seems to be entirely within the limits of known facts while attempting to deal with them. We believe it will give all thoughtful bee-keepers a greater liking for their business to read it. Probably it has more to do with the curious traditions connected with bees than any other book of the kind. Price $1.50 postpaid.

THE LIFE OF THE BEE. By Maeterlinck. This is a masterpiece of fine writing by a modern Shakespeare. The words fly from the pen of this writer like sparks from a blacksmith's anvil, the result being a glorification of the honey-bee. Maeterlinck is considered by many to be the finest writer now living, and anything from him is sure to be worth reading. He is, to a certain extent, familiar with bee-keeping, but the truth about bees does not interest him so much as the romance of the queen and the drone and the swarming instinct. The book itself is well bound and beautifully printed. Price $1.40 postpaid.

THE BEE PEOPLE. A book on bees, especially for children, from the pen of Margaret W. Morley. Including its elegant illustrations, it is in some respects, the prettiest bee-book in existence. It has 177 pages, very coarse print, the reading being ingeniously interwoven with the illustrations showing the parts of the bee. The story of bee-life is told in a fascinating manner, and is well calculated to get the casual reader, as well as children, interested in this useful insect. The cuts go just enough into detail to explain fully the lesson taught, without confusing the mind with other things. We think the book well worthy a place in every bee-keeper's home. Fittingly designed cover. Price $1.50 postpaid.

THE LORE OF THE HONEY-BEE. By Tickner Edwards. A fine work for those who desire an interesting book about bees. Does not deal with practical details, but gives valuable information about bees in general. Very readable and entertaining. Price $2.00 postpaid.

THE GLEANINGS LIBRARY.

So called because of great popularity of the following books when offered in combination with Gleanings in Bee Culture.

ALEXANDER'S WRITINGS ON PRACTICAL BEE CULTURE. By the late E. W. Alexander, who conducted the largest apiary in the United States. A wonderfully interesting discussion of bee-keeping in its broadest phases. Any one can understand it. 35 chapters, 95 pages. Paper bound, 50 cts. postpaid.

A YEAR'S WORK IN AN OUT-APIARY. By G. M. Doolittle. Packed full of most valuable information ever given to bee-keepers. A practical and interesting book by a very successful apiarist. Sale has reached nearly 5,000 copies. 60 pages, paper bound, 50 cts. postpaid.

THE TOWNSEND BEE BOOK. By E. D. Townsend. Written by one of the most progressive, successful and extensive bee-keepers in the U. S. this new book has been in great demand from the day of its announcement. Tells how to make a start with bees, and will greatly benefit beginners and experienced bee-keepers. 90 pages, paper bound, 50 cts. postpaid.

In Combination With Gleanings in Bee Culture for One Year either of the above Books may be had for the price of Gleanings alone, $1. Foreign postage 60 cts. extra. Canadian postage 30 cts. extra.

THE BEE-KEEPERS' TEN-CENT LIBRARY.

The following books are neatly bound in paper, well illustrated. Just the thing for beginners to help them with their troubles. Price 10 cts. each postpaid.

No. 1. **BEE-KEEPERS' DICTIONARY.** It helps a beginner or one who is not acquainted with the literature of beekeeping to understand the different terms used by writers on the subject. A reference work giving clear definitions of current terms.

No. 5. **TRANSFERRING BEES.** Practical methods of transferring from boxes to modern hives.

No. 11. **WINTERING BEES.** The problems of wintering bees in different localities and suggestions for their solution.

No. 16. **MODERN QUEEN-REARING.** Detailing the latest methods, by leading breeders, embracing the best of several systems.

No. 17. **HABITS OF THE HONEY-BEE.** A condensed account of the life and habits of the bee in simple language.

No. 21. **FACTS ABOUT BEES.** Just what its name indicates. A very popular booklet of 60 pages containing a complete description of the Danzenbaker hive, and instructions for its management.

No. 29. **MOVING AND SHIPPING BEES.** Full of helpful suggestions on a subject in which many bee-keepers are interested.

No. 30. **THE BEE-KEEPER AND THE FRUIT-GROWER.** Why and how their interests are mutual.

These books may be obtained from the publishers of this volume or from dealers in bee-keepers' supplies everywhere.

www.ingramcontent.com/pod-product-compliance
Lightning Source LLC
Chambersburg PA
CBHW081419270326
41931CB00015B/3335